D0853388

A Scots Sampler

An Anthology of Prose and Verse

COMPILED BY

W. R. KERMACK

This edition published by Barnes & Noble, Inc.

1993 Barnes & Noble Books

ISBN 1-56619-129-7

Printed and bound in the United States of America

M 9 8 7 6 5 4 3 2 1

CONTENTS

ACKNOWLEDGMENT

To Dr. R. F. Rattray, Cambridge, the publishers are indebted for advice regarding the contents of this book, and for his contribution of Scots stories.

1. Characters

THE MANSE

I HAVE named, among many rivers that make music in my memory, that dirty Water of Leith. Often and often I desire to look upon it again; and the choice of a point of view is easy to me. It should be at a certain water-door, embowered in shrubbery. The river is there dammed back for the service of the flour-mill just below, so that it lies deep and darkling, and the sand slopes into brown obscurity with a glint of gold; and it has but newly been recruited by the borrowings of the snuff-mill just above, and these, tumbling merrily in, shake the pool to its black heart, fill it with drowsy eddies, and set the curded froth of many other mills solemnly steering to and fro upon the surface. Or so it was when I was young; for change, and the masons, and the pruning-knife, have been busy; and if I could hope to repeat a cherished experience, it must be on many and impossible conditions. I must choose, as well as the point of view, a certain moment in my growth, so that the scale may be exaggerated, and the trees on the steep opposite side may seem to climb to heaven, and the sand by the water-door, where I am standing, seem as low as Styx. And I must choose the season also, so that the valley may be brimmed like a cup with sunshine and the songs of birds;—and the year of grace, so that when I turn to leave the riverside I may find the old manse and its inhabitants unchanged.

It was a place in that time like no other: the garden cut into provinces by a great hedge of beech, and overlooked by the church and the terrace of the churchyard, where the tombstones were thick, and after nightfall " spunkies " might be seen to dance, at least by children ; flower-plots lying warm in sunshine ; laurels and the great yew making elsewhere a pleasing horror of shade ; the smell of water rising from all round, with an added tang of paper-mills ; the sound of water everywhere, and the sound of mills—the wheel and the dam singing their alternate strain ; the birds on every bush and from every corner of the overhanging woods pealing out their notes until the air throbbed with them ; and in the midst of this, the manse. I see it, by the standard of my childish stature, as a great and roomy house. In truth, it was not so large as I supposed, nor yet so convenient, and, standing where it did, it is difficult to suppose that it was healthful. Yet a large family of stalwart sons and tall daughters was housed and reared, and came to man and womanhood in that nest of little chambers ; so that the face of the earth was peppered with the children of the manse, and letters with outlandish stamps became familiar to the local postman, and the walls of the little chambers brightened with the wonders of the East. The dullest could see this was a house that had a pair of hands in divers foreign places : a well-beloved house—its image fondly dwelt on by many travellers.

Here lived an ancestor of mine, who was a herd of men. I read him, judging with older criticism the report of childish observation, as a man of singular simplicity of nature ; unemotional, and hating the display of what he felt ; standing contented on the old ways ; a lover of his life and innocent habits to the end. We children admired him : partly for his beautiful face and silver hair, for none more than children are concerned for beauty and, above all, for beauty in the old ; partly for the solemn light in which we beheld him once a week, the observed of all observers, in the pulpit. But his strictness and distance, the effect, I now fancy, of old age, slow blood, and settled habit, oppressed us with a kind of terror. When not abroad, he sat much alone, writing sermons or letters to his scattered family in a dark and cold room with a library of bloodless books—or so they seemed in those days, although I have some of them now on my own shelves and like well enough to read them ; and these lonely hours wrapped him in the greater gloom for our imaginations. But the study had a redeeming grace in many Indian pictures, gaudily coloured and dear to young eyes. I cannot depict (for I have no such passions now) the greed with which I beheld them ; and when I was once sent in to say a psalm to my grandfather, I went, quaking indeed with fear, but at the same time glowing with hope that, if I said it well, he might reward me with an Indian picture.

"Thy foot He'll not let slide, nor will
He slumber that thee keeps,"

it ran : a strange conglomerate of the unpronounceable, a sad model to set in childhood before one who was himself to be a versifier, and a task in recitation that really merited reward. And I must suppose the old man thought so too, and was either touched or amused by the performance ; for he took me in his arms with most unwonted tenderness, and kissed me, and gave me a little kindly sermon for my psalm ; so that, for that day, we were clerk and parson. I was struck by this reception into so tender a surprise that I forgot my disappointment. And indeed the hope was one of those that childhood forges for a pastime, and with no design upon reality. Nothing was more unlikely than that my grandfather should strip himself of one of those pictures, love-gifts and reminders of his absent sons ; nothing more unlikely than that he should bestow it upon me. He had no idea of spoiling children, leaving all that to my aunt ; he had fared hard himself, and blubbered under the rod in the last century ; and his ways were still Spartan for the young. The last word I heard upon his lips was in this Spartan key. He had overwalked in the teeth of an east wind, and was now near the end of his many days. He sat by the dining-room fire, with his white hair, pale face and bloodshot eyes, a somewhat awful figure ; and my aunt had given him a dose of our good old Scotch medicine, Dr. Gregory's powder. Now that remedy, as the work of a near kinsman of Rob Roy himself, may have a savour of romance for the imagination ; but it comes uncouthly to the palate. The old gentleman had taken it with a wry face ; and that being accomplished, sat with perfect simplicity, like a child's, munching a " barley-sugar kiss." But when my aunt, having the canister open in her hands, proposed to let me share in the sweets, he interfered at once. I had had no Gregory ; then I should have no barley-sugar kiss : so he decided with a touch of irritation. And just then the phaeton coming opportunely to the kitchen door—for such was our unlordly fashion —I was taken for the last time from the presence of my grandfather. . . .

Robert Louis Stevenson.
(From *Memories and Portraits.*)

DONALD CAIRD

Donald Caird's come again! — caird = tinker
Donald Caird's come again!
Tell the news in brugh and glen, — burgh
Donald Caird's come again.

Donald Caird can lilt and sing,
Blithely dance the Hieland fling,
Drink till the gudeman be blind,
Fleech till the gudewife be kind;
Hoop a leglin, clout a pan, — milk-pail; mend
Or crack a pow wi' ony man;— — head
Tell the news in brugh and glen,
Donald Caird's come again.

Donald Caird's come again!
Donald Caird's come again!
Tell the news in brugh and glen,
Donald Caird's come again.

Donald Caird can wire a maukin, — hare
Kens the wiles o' dun-deer staukin',
Leisters kipper, makes a shift — catches fish
To shoot a muir-fowl in the drift;
Water-bailiffs, rangers, keepers,—
He can wauk when they are sleepers; — wake
Nor for bountith or rewaird
Dare ye mell wi' Donald Caird. — meddle

Donald Caird's come again!
Donald Caird's come again!
Gar the bagpipes hum amain,
Donald Caird's come again.

Donald Caird can drink a gill
Fast as hostler-wife can fill;
Ilka ane that sells gude liquor — everyone
Kens how Donald bends a bicker; — drinks a bowl

When he's fou he's stout and saucy,
crown of the causeway Keeps the cantle o' the causey;
Hieland chief and Lawland laird
Maun gie room to Donald Caird!

Donald Caird's come again!
Donald Caird's come again!
Tell the news in brugh and glen,
Donald Caird's come again.

shut; cupboard; chest Steek the amrie, lock the kist,
Else some gear may weel be mis't;
miscellaneous Donald Caird finds orra things
tongs Where Allan Gregor fand the tings;
slices of cheese; hanks of wool Dunts of kebbuck, taits o' woo,
sometimes Whiles a hen and whiles a sow,
clothes Web or duds frae hedge or yaird—
hangman's rope 'Ware the wuddie, Donald Caird!

Donald Caird's come again!
Donald Caird's come again!
Sheriff Dinna let the Shirra ken
Donald Caird's come again.

On Donald Caird the doom was stern,
neck; iron Craig to tether, legs to airn;
But Donald Caird, wi' mickle study,
Caught the gift to cheat the wuddie;
Rings of airn, and bolts of steel,
Fell like ice frae hand and heel!
Watch the sheep in fauld and glen,
Donald Caird's come again!

Donald Caird's come again!
Donald Caird's come again!
Dinna let the Justice ken,
Donald Caird's come again.

SIR WALTER SCOTT.

2. *Humour*

LAST MAY A BRAW WOOER

Last May a braw wooer cam' down the lang glen,
And sair wi' his love he did deave me ; sore ; deafen
I said, there was naething I hated like men,
The deuce gae wi' him to believe me, believe me,
The deuce gae wi' him, to believe me.

He spak' o' the darts in my bonnie black een, eyes
And vow'd for my love he was dying ;
I said he might die when he liket for Jean,
The Lord forgi'e me for lying, for lying,
The Lord forgi'e me for lying !

A weel-stocked mailin—himsel' for the laird— farm
And marriage aff-hand were his proffers :
I never loot on that I kend it, or car'd, let ; knew
But thought I might hae waur offers, waur offers, worse
But thought I might hae waur offers.

But what wad ye think ? in a fortnight or less—
The de'il tak' his taste to gae near her !
He up the lang loan to my black cousin Bess, road
Guess ye how the jad ! I could bear her, could bear her,
Guess ye how the jad ! I could bear her.

next — But a' the niest week as I petted wi' care,
fair — I gaed to the tryste o' Dalgarnock,
And wha but my fine fickle lover was there!
stared — I glowr'd as I'd seen a warlock, a warlock,
I glowr'd as I'd seen a warlock.

But owre my left shouther I ga'e him a blink,
Lest neebours might say I was saucy;
My wooer he caper'd as he'd been in drink,
And vow'd I was his dear lassie, dear lassie,
And vow'd I was his dear lassie.

asked; gracious — I speir'd for my cousin fu' couthy and sweet,
If she had recover'd her hearing;
shapeless — And how her new shoon fit her auld shachl't feet,
But heavens! how he fell a-swearing, a-swearing,
But heavens! how he fell a-swearing.

He begged, for gude-sake, I wad be his wife,
Or else I wad kill him with sorrow;
So e'en to preserve the poor body his life,
I think I maun wed him—to-morrow, to-morrow,
I think I maun wed him to-morrow.

ROBERT BURNS.

SCOTS STORIES

An American, being shown things in Scotland by a Glasgow man, hurt him by repeatedly saying that they had bigger and better in the United States. When they came to Loch Katrine, the American was for the first time impressed and said, " Yes, it's a mighty fine lake : I like it." " Well," said the Scot, gaining some confidence, " do you know that in the year 1886 we put down pipes and laid this water on to Glasgow ? " " That gives me an idea," said the American : " I guess we've gat engineers on the other side who could put pipes acrass the Atlantic and lay this water on to Noo Yark : do you think the water would come through ? " " Weel," said the Scot, " if you chaps ower there are as guid at sookin' as ye are at blawin', ye'll get the water a' richt."

An Englishman candidating in a Scottish constituency, when submitting to heckling, was confronted by a voter who said in a rather contemptuous tone, " Ye're an Englishman, aren't ye ? " The candidate was stung and replied, with spirit, " Yes, sir, I *am* an Englishman : I was born an Englishman and I hope to die an Englishman." " Man," said the Scot, " hiv' ye nae ambeetion ? "

A Swiss, naturalised in England, called de Paravicini, went to play golf at St. Andrews for the first time. He went up to the starter's box and said, " Put me down for ten o'clock to-morrow morning. The name is de Paravicini." The old Scot in the box did not raise his head and the visitor repeated the request twice. Then the Scottish head rose and said, " Ye'll come the day efter the morn at eleeven and ye'll answer tae the name o' Macpherson."

The late Sir D'Arcy Thompson one Saturday night found himself in a crowded tramcar opposite a drunk man. To his horror, the latter proceeded to address him in a loud voice. "A ken ye, Professor Thoampson, A ken ye." "Yes, yes," said Thompson hastily, "I dare say, I dare say." "Ay, ye're a cliver man, Professor Thoampson, but A ken something that you dinna ken—A'm wearin' yin o' yer shurts: ma wife washes fur ye."

Clerical

Non-Scots are generally unaware of the importance of the part played in Scottish life by the Church. Scots have taken an intense interest in ministers ; many have been connoisseurs of preaching and sometimes outspoken critics.

A minister, preaching in a strange church, before the morning service asked the beadle, " At what point in the service do I give out the intimations ? " " O," said the beadle, " we only give out the intimations at the evening service here." During singing after the sermon the beadle came up the pulpit steps, handed the minister some papers and whispered, " Ye'd better gie oot the intimations." " But," whispered back the minister, " you said that you only gave out the intimations at the evening service." " Ay," replied the beadle, " but A doot there'll no be much o' an evenin' service the nicht."

Another story of a minister preaching in a strange church is that, during his sermon, a man in the congregation got up and walked out. After service the minister asked the beadle, " Did you see that man get up and walk out during the sermon? Was he ill or was it intentional rudeness?" "O," said the beadle, "him? O, that's a' richt. He's what they ca' a somnambulist."

Another story of the crushing of a minister is of a "candidate" who after the first service was anxious to find out what sort of impression he had made and asked the beadle. "Nae yiss ava," (no use at all), was the reply. "Dear me," said the discomfited candidate, "do you mind telling me what was wrong with my sermon?" "Weel, in the furst place, it was read; secondly, it was badly read; and in the thurd place, it wisna worth readin'."

On the side of the minister:—A living minister of a city parish went district-visiting among the unconverted. At one door a woman said, "A ken ye. Ye're frae Ruchill. I wudnae set fit in that kirk: it's fu' o' hypocreets." "Madam," said the minister, "there is room for one more."

In the old days ministers did not mince matters. One in the course of a sermon said, "A've kent o' better folk than you, efter they were deed, in the place where the wurm dieth not and the fire is not quenched, callin' out tae the Lord in their agony, 'O Lord, A niver kent it wud be as bad as this.' And the Lord, out of His love and tender mercy vouchsafed the answer, 'Weel, ye ken noo.'"

A minister with very High Church tendencies, preaching at a strange church, took his vestments with him, much to the disgust of the beadle. "Pass me my cincture," said the minister. "Yer whaat?" asked the beadle. The minister pointed and repeated, "Pass me my cincture." "O," said the beadle, "it's yer bellyband ye want!"

3. *Enchantment*

KILMENY

BONNY Kilmeny gaed up the glen,
But it wasna to meet Duneira's men,
Nor the rosy monk of the isle to see,
For Kilmeny was pure as pure could be.
yellow-hammer It was only to hear the yorlin sing,
And pu' the cress-flower round the spring;
raspberry The scarlet hypp and the hindberrye,
And the nut that hung frae the hazel tree;
For Kilmeny was pure as pure could be.
mother But lang may her minny look o'er the wa',
And lang may she seek i' the green-wood shaw;
Lang the laird o' Duneira blame,
weep And lang, lang greet or Kilmeny come hame!

When many a day had come and fled,
When grief grew calm, and hope was dead,
When mass for Kilmeny's soul had been sung,
When the bedesman had prayed, and the
dead bell rung,
Late, late in a gloamin' when all was still,
When the fringe was red on the westlin' hill,
The wood was sere, the moon i' the wane,
smoke The reek o' the cot hung over the plain,
alone Like a little wee cloud in the world its lane;
fire burned with an eerie light When the ingle lowed with an eiry leme—
Late, late in the gloamin' Kilmeny came
hame!

"Kilmeny, Kilmeny, where have you been?
Lang hae we sought baith holt and dean; glen
By linn, by ford, and green-wood tree,
Yet you are halesome and fair to see.
Where gat you that joup o' the lily schene? petticoat
That bonny snood of the birk sae green? hair-band
And these roses, the fairest that ever were seen?
Kilmeny, Kilmeny, where have you been?"

Kilmeny looked up wi' a lovely grace,
But nae smile was seen on Kilmeny's face;
As still was her look, and as still was her ee,
As the stillness that lay on the emerant lea, emerald
Or the mist that sleeps on a waveless sea.
For Kilmeny had been she knew not where,
And Kilmeny had seen what she could not declare;
Kilmeny had been where the cock never crew,
Where the rain never fell, and the wind never blew;
But it seemed as the harp of the sky had rung,
And the airs of heaven played round her tongue,
When she spake of the lovely forms she had seen,
And a land where sin had never been;
A land of love, and a land of light,
Withouten sun, or moon, or night;
Where the river swa'd a living stream, swelled
And the light a pure celestial beam:
The land of vision it would seem,
A still, an everlasting dream. . . .

When a month and a day had come and gane,
nook — Kilmeny sought the green-wood wene ;
There laid her down on the leaves sae green,
And Kilmeny on earth was never mair seen. . . .
It wasna her hame, and she couldna remain ;
She left this world of sorrow and pain,
And returned to the land of thought again.

JAMES HOGG.

PROUD MAISIE

PROUD Maisie is in the wood,
Walking so early ;
Sweet Robin sits on the bush,
Singing so rarely.

" Tell me, thou bonny bird,
When shall I marry me ? "
" When six braw gentlemen
Kirkward shall carry ye."

" Who makes the bridal bed,
Birdie, say truly ? "
" The grey-headed sexton
That delves the grave duly.

" The glow-worm o'er grave and stone
Shall light thee steady ;
The owl from the steeple sing,
' Welcome, proud lady '."

SIR WALTER SCOTT.

4. *Witches and Warlocks*

WANDERING WILLIE'S TALE

YE maun have heard of Sir Robert Redgauntlet of that Ilk, who lived in these parts before the dear years. The country will lang mind him; and our fathers used to draw breath thick if ever they heard him named. He was out wi' the Hielandmen in Montrose's time, and again he was in the hills wi' Glencairn in the saxteen hundred and fifty-twa; and sae when King Charles the Second came in, wha was in sic favour as the Laird of Redgauntlet? He was knighted at Lonon court, wi' the King's ain sword; and, being a redhot Prelatist, he came down here, rampauging like a lion, with commissions of lieutenancy (and of lunacy, for what I ken), to put down a' the Whigs and Covenanters in the country. Wild wark they made of it; for the Whigs were as dour as Cavaliers were fierce, and it was which should first tire the other. Redgauntlet was aye for the strong hand; and his name is kend as wide in the country as Claverhouse's or Tam Dalyell's. Glen, nor dargle, nor mountain, nor cave, could hide the puir hill-folk when Redgauntlet was out with bugle and bloodhound after them, as if they had been sae mony deer. And troth when they fand them, they didna mak muckle mair ceremony than a Hielandman wi' a roebuck. It was just, "Will ye tak the test?" If not, "Make ready—present—fire!"—and there lay the recusant.

Far and wide was Sir Robert hated and feared.

Men thought he had a direct compact with Satan—that he was proof against steel—and that bullets happed aff his buff-coat like hailstanes from a hearth—that he had a mear that would turn a hare on the the side of Carrifra-gawns[1]—and muckle to the same purpose, of whilk mair anon. The best blessing they wared on him was, " Deil scowp wi' Redgauntlet ! " He wasna a bad maister to his ain folk though, and was weel aneugh liked by his tenants ; and as for the lackeys and troopers that rade out wi' him to the persecutions, as the Whigs caa'd those killing times, they wad hae drunken themsells blind to his health at ony time.

Now you are to ken that my gudesire lived on Redgauntlet's grund—they ca' the place Primrose Knowe. We had lived on the grund, and under the Redgauntlets, since the riding days, and lang before. It was a pleasant bit ; and I think the air is callerer and fresher there than ony where else in the country. It's a' deserted now ; and I sat on the broken door-cheek three days since, and was glad I couldna see the plight the place was in ; but that's a' wide o' the mark. There dwelt my gudesire, Steenie Steenson, a rambling, rattling chiel he had been in his young days, and could play weel on the pipes ; he was famous at " Hoopers and Girders "—a' Cumberland couldna touch him at " Jockie Lattin "—and he had the finest finger for the backlilt between Berwick and Carlisle. The like o' Steenie wasna the sort that they made Whigs o'. And so he became a Tory, as they ca' it, which we now ca' Jacobites, just out of a kind of needcessity, that he might belang to some side or other. He had nae ill will to the Whig bodies, and liked little to see the blude rin, though, being obliged to follow Sir Robert in

[1] A precipitous side of a mountain in Moffatdale.

hunting and hosting, watching and warding, he saw muckle mischief, and maybe did some, that he couldna avoid.

Now Steenie was a kind of favourite with his master, and kend a' the folks about the Castle, and was often sent for to play the pipes when they were at their merriment. Auld Dougal MacCallum, the butler, that had followed Sir Robert through gude and ill, thick and thin, pool and stream, was specially fond of the pipes, and aye gae my gudesire his gude word wi' the Laird ; for Dougal could turn his master round his finger.

Weel, round came the Revolution, and it had like to have broken the hearts baith of Dougal and his master. But the change was not a'thegither sae great as they feared, and other folk thought for. The Whigs made an unco crawing what they wad do with their auld enemies, and in special wi' Sir Robert Redgauntlet. But there were ower mony great folks dipped in the same doings, to mak a spick and span new warld. So Parliament passed it a' ower easy ; and Sir Robert, bating that he was held to hunting foxes instead of Covenanters, remained just the man he was. His revel was as loud, and his hall as weel lighted, as ever it had been, though maybe he lacked the fines of the nonconformists, that used to come to stock his larder and cellar ; for it is certain he began to be keener about the rents than his tenants used to find him before, and they behoved to be prompt to the rent-day, or else the Laird wasna pleased. And he was sic an awesome body, that naebody cared to anger him ; for the oaths he swore, and the rage that he used to get into, and the looks that he put on, made men sometimes think him a devil incarnate.

Weel, my gudesire was nae manager—no that he

was a very great misguider—but he hadna the saving gift, and he got twa terms' rent in arrear. He got the first brash at Whitsunday put ower wi' fair word and piping ; but when Martinmas came, there was a summons from the grund-officer to come wi' the rent on a day preceese, or else Steenie behoved to flit. Sair wark he had to get the siller ; but he was weel-freended, and at last he got the haill scraped thegither—a thousand merks—the maist of it was from a neighbour they caa'd Laurie Lapraik—a sly tod. Laurie had walth o' gear—could hunt wi' the hound and rin wi' the hare—and be Whig or Tory, saunt or sinner, as the wind stood. He was a professor in this Revolution warld, but he liked an orra sough of this warld, and a tune on the pipes weel eneugh at a bytime, and abune a', he thought he had a gude security for the siller he lent my gudesire ower the stocking at Primrose Knowe.

Away trots my gudesire to Redgauntlet Castle, wi' a heavy purse and a light heart, glad to be out of the Laird's danger. Weel, the first thing he learned at the Castle was, that Sir Robert had fretted himsell into a fit of the gout, because he did not appear before twelve o'clock. It wasna a'thegither for sake of the money, Dougal thought ; but because he didna like to part wi' my gudesire aff the grund. Dougal was glad to see Steenie, and brought him into the great oak parlour, and there sat the Laird his leesome lain, excepting that he had beside him a great, ill-favoured jackanape, that was a special pet of his ; a cankered beast it was, and mony an ill-natured trick it played—ill to please it was, and easily angered—ran about the haill castle—chattering and yowling, and pinching, and biting folk, especially before ill weather, or disturbances in the state. Sir Robert caa'd it Major

Weir [1], after the warlock that was burnt, and few folk liked either the name or the conditions of the creature —they thought there was something in it by ordinar— and my gudesire was not just easy in his mind when the door shut on him, and he saw himself in the room wi' naebody but the Laird, Dougal MacCallum, and the Major, a thing that hadna chanced to him before.

Sir Robert sat, or, I should say, lay, in a great armed chair, wi' his grand velvet gown, and his feet on a cradle ; for he had baith gout and gravel, and his face looked as gash and ghastly as Satan's. Major Weir sat opposite to him, in a red laced coat, and the Laird's wig on his head ; and aye as Sir Robert girned wi' pain, the jackanape girned too, like a sheep's-head between a pair of tangs—an ill-faur'd, fearsome couple they were. The Laird's buff-coat was hung on a pin behind him, and his broadsword and his pistols within reach ; for he keepit up the auld fashion of having the weapons ready, and a horse saddled day and night, just as he used to do when he was able to loup on horseback, and away after ony of the hill-folk he could get speerings of. Some said it was for fear of the Whigs taking vengeance, but I judge it was just his auld custom—he wasna gien to fear ony thing. The rental-book, wi' its black cover and brass clasps, was lying beside him ; and a book of sculduddry sangs was put betwixt the leaves, to keep it open at the place where it bore evidence against the Goodman of Primrose Knowe, as behind the hand with his mails and duties. Sir Robert gave my gudesire a look, as if he would have withered his heart in his bosom. Ye maun ken he had a way of bending his brows, that men saw the

[1] A celebrated wizard, executed at Edinburgh for sorcery and other crimes.

visible mark of a horse-shoe in his forehead, deep dinted, as if it had been stamped there.

"Are ye come light-handed, ye son of a toom whistle?" said Sir Robert. "Zounds! if you are——"

My gudesire, with as gude a countenance as he could put on, made a leg, and placed the bag of money on the table wi' a dash, like a man that does something clever. The Laird drew it to him hastily—"Is it all here, Steenie, man?"

"Your honour will find it right," said my gudesire.

"Here, Dougal," said the Laird, "gie Steenie a tass of brandy downstairs, till I count the siller and write the receipt."

But they werena weel out of the room, when Sir Robert gied a yelloch that garr'd the Castle rock. Back ran Dougal—in flew the livery men—yell on yell gied the Laird, ilk ane mair aefu' than the ither. My gudesire knew not whether to stand or flee, but he ventured back into the parlour, where a' was gaun hirdy-girdie—naebody to say "come in," or "gae out." Terribly the Laird roared for cauld water to his feet, and wine to cool his throat; and hell, hell, hell, and its flames, was aye the word in his mouth. They brought him water, and when they plunged his swollen feet into the tub, he cried out it was burning; and folk say that it *did* bubble and sparkle like a seething caldron. He flung the cup at Dougal's head, and said he had given him blood instead of burgundy; and, sure aneugh, the lass washed clotted blood aff the carpet the neist day. The jackanape they caa'd Major Weir, it jibbered and cried as if it was mocking its master, my gudesire's head was like to turn—he forgot baith siller and receipt, and downstairs he banged; but as he ran, the shrieks came faint and fainter; there was a deep-drawn shivering groan, and word gaed through the Castle that the Laird was dead.

Weel, away come my gudesire, wi' his finger in his mouth, and his best hope was that Dougal had seen the money-bag, and heard the Laird speak of writing the receipt. The young Laird, now Sir John, came from Edinburgh, to see things put to rights. Sir John and his father never gree'd weel. Sir John had been bred an advocate, and afterwards sat in the last Scots Parliament and voted for the Union, having gotten, it was thought, a rug of the compensations—if his father could have come out of his grave, he would have brained him for it on his awn hearthstane. Some thought it was easier counting with the auld rough Knight than the fair-spoken young ane—but mair of that anon.

Dougal MacCallum, poor body, neither grat nor graned, but gaed about the house looking like a corpse, but directing, as was his duty, a' the order of the grand funeral. Now, Dougal looked aye waur and waur when night was coming, and was aye the last to gang to his bed, whilk was in a little round just opposite the chamber of dais, whilk his master occupied while he was living, and where he now lay in state, as they caa'd it, weel-a-day! The night before the funeral, Dougal could keep his awn counsel nae langer; he cam doun with his proud spirit, and fairly asked auld Hutcheon to sit in his room with him for an hour. When they were in the round, Dougal took ae tass of brandy to himsell, and gave another to Hutcheon, and wished him all health and lang life, and said that, for himsell, he wasna lang for this world; for that, every night since Sir Robert's death, his silver call had sounded from the state-chamber, just as it used to do at nights in his lifetime, to call Dougal to help to turn him in his bed. Dougal said that, being alone with the dead on that floor of the tower (for naebody cared to wake Sir Robert Redgauntlet like another corpse), he had never daured to answer the call, but that now his conscience checked him for neglecting his duty; for, "though death breaks service," said MacCallum, "it shall never break my service to Sir Robert; and I will answer his next whistle, so be you will stand by me, Hutcheon."

Hutcheon had nae will to the wark, but he had stood by Dougal in battle and broil, and he wad not fail him at this pinch; so down the carles sat ower a stoup of brandy, and Hutcheon, who was something of a clerk, would have read a chapter of the Bible; but Dougal would hear naething but a blaud of Davie Lindsay, whilk was the waur preparation.

When midnight came, and the house was quiet as the grave, sure aneugh the silver whistle sounded as sharp and shrill as if Sir Robert was blowing it, and up gat the twa auld serving-men, and tottered into the room where the dead man lay. Hutcheon saw aneugh at the first glance; for there were torches in the room, which showed him the foul fiend, in his ain shape, sitting on the Laird's coffin! Over he cowped as if he had been dead. He could not tell how lang he lay in a trance at the door, but when he gathered himself, he cried on his neighbour, and, getting nae answer, raised the house, when Dougal was found lying dead within twa steps of the bed where his master's coffin was placed. As for the whistle, it was gaen anes and aye; but mony a time was it heard at the top of the house on the bartizan, and amang the auld chimneys and turrets, where the howlets have their nests. Sir John hushed the matter up, and the funeral passed over without mair bogle-wark.

But when a' was ower, and the Laird was beginning to settle his affairs, every tenant was called up for his arrears, and my gudesire for the full sum that stood against him in the rental book. Weel, away he trots to the Castle, to tell his story, and there he is introduced to Sir John, sitting in his father's chair, in deep mourning, with weepers and hanging cravat, and a small walking rapier by his side, instead of the auld broadsword, that had a hundredweight of steel about it, what with blade, chape, and basket-hilt. I have heard their communing so often tauld ower that I almost think I was there mysell, though I couldna be born at the time. [My gudesire] had, while he spoke, his eye fixed on the rental-book, as if it were a mastiff-dog that he was afraid would spring up and bite him.

" I wuss ye joy, sir, of the head seat, and the white loaf, and the braid lairdship. Your father was a kind man to friends and followers; muckle grace to you, Sir John, to fill his shoon—his boots, I suld say, for he seldom wore shoon, unless it were muils when he had the gout."

" Ay, Steenie," quoth the Laird, sighing deeply and putting his napkin to his een, " his was a sudden call, and he will be missed in the country; no time to set his house in order—weel prepared Godward, no doubt, which is the root of the matter—but left us behind a tangled hesp to wind, Steenie. Hem! hem! We maun go to business, Steenie; much to do, and little time to do it in."

Here he opened the fatal volume. I have heard of a thing they call Doomsday-book—I am clear it has been a rental of back-ganging tenants.

" Stephen," said Sir John, still in the same soft, sleekit tone of voice—" Stephen Stevenson, or Steenson, ye are down here for a year's rent behind the hand—due at last term."

Stephen. " Please your honour, Sir John, I paid it to your father."

Sir John. " Ye took a receipt then, doubtless, Stephen ; and can produce it ? "

Stephen. " Indeed I hadna time, an it like your honour ; for nae sooner had I set doun the siller, and just as his honour Sir Robert, that's gaen, drew it till him to count it, and write out the receipt, he was ta'en wi' the pains that removed him."

" That was unlucky," said Sir John, after a pause. " But ye maybe paid it in the presence of somebody. I want but a *talis qualis* evidence, Stephen. I would go ower strictly to work with no poor man."

Stephen. " Troth, Sir John, there was naebody in the room but Dougal MacCallum the butler. But, as your honour kens, he has e'en followed his auld master."

" Very unlucky again, Stephen," said Sir John, without altering his voice a single note. " The man to whom ye paid the money is dead—and the man who witnessed the payment is dead too—and the siller, which should have been to the fore, is neither seen nor heard tell of in the repositories. How am I to believe a' this ? "

Stephen. " I dinna ken, your honour ; but there is a bit memorandum note of the very coins ; for, God help me ! I had to borrow out of twenty purses ; and I am sure that ilka man there set down will take his grit oath for what purpose I borrowed the money."

Sir John. " I have little doubt ye *borrowed* the money, Steenie. It is the *payment* to my father that I want to have some proof of."

Stephen. " The siller maun be about the house, Sir John. And since your honour never got it, and his honour that was canna have ta'en it wi' him, maybe some of the family may have seen it."

Sir John. "We will examine the servants, Stephen; that is but reasonable."

But lackey and lass, and page and groom, all denied stoutly that they had ever seen such a bag of money as my gudesire described. What was waur, he had unluckily not mentioned to any living soul of them his purpose of paying his rent. Ae quean had noticed something under his arm, but she took it for the pipes.

Sir John Redgauntlet ordered the servants out of the room, and then said to my gudesire, "Now, Steenie, ye see you have fair play; and as I have little doubt ye ken better where to find the siller than ony other body, I beg, in fair terms, and for your own sake, that you will end this fasherie; for, Stephen, ye maun pay or flit."

"The Lord forgie your opinion," said Stephen, driven almost to his wit's end—"I am an honest man."

"So am I, Stephen," said his honour, "and so are all the folks in this house, I hope. But if there be a knave amongst us, it must be he that tells the story he cannot prove." He paused, and then added, mair sternly, "If I understand your trick, sir, you want to take advantage of some malicious reports concerning things in this family, and particularly respecting my father's sudden death, thereby to cheat me out of the money, and perhaps take away my character, by insinuating that I have received the rent I am demanding. Where do you suppose this money to be? I insist upon knowing."

My gudesire saw everything look sae muckle against him that he grew nearly desperate—however, he shifted from one foot to another, looked to every corner of the room, and made no answer.

"Speak out, sirrah," said the Laird, assuming a look of his father's, a very particular ane, which he had when he was angry—it seemed as if the wrinkles of his frown made that self-same fearful shape of a horse's shoe in the middle of his brow. "Speak out, sir! I *will* know your thoughts; do you suppose that I have this money?"

"Far be it frae me to say so," said Stephen.

"Do you charge any of my people with having taken it?"

"I wad be laith to charge them that may be innocent," said my gudesire; "and if there be any one that is guilty, I have nae proof."

"Somewhere the money must be, if there is a word of truth in your story," said Sir John; "I ask where you think it is—and demand a correct answer?"

"In hell, if you *will* have my thoughts of it," said my gudesire, driven to extremity—"in hell! with your father, his jackanape, and his silver whistle."

Down the stairs he ran (for the parlour was nae place for him after such a word), and he heard the Laird swearing blood and wounds behind him, as fast as ever did Sir Robert, and roaring for the bailie and the baron-officer.

Away rode my gudesire to his chief creditor (him they caa'd Laurie Lapraik), to try if he could make ony thing out of him; but when he tauld his story, he got but the warst word in his wame—thief, beggar, and dyvour, were the saftest terms; and to the boot of these hard terms, Laurie brought up the auld story of his dipping his hand in the blood of God's saunts, just as if a tenant could have helped riding with the Laird, and that a laird like Sir Robert Redgauntlet. My gudesire was, by this time, far beyond the bounds of patience, and while he and Laurie were at deil speed the liars, he was wanchancie aneugh to abuse Lapraik's doctrine as weel as the man, and said things that garr'd folk's flesh grue that heard them ; he wasna just himsell, and he had lived wi' a wild set in his day.

At last they parted, and my gudesire was to ride hame through the wood of Pitmurkie—that is a' fou of black firs, as they say. I ken the wood, but the firs may be black or white for what I can tell. At the entry of the wood there is a wild common, and on the edge of the common, a little lonely change-house, that was keepit then by an ostler-wife, they suld hae caa'd her Tibbie Faw, and there puir Steenie cried for a mutchkin of brandy, for he had had no refreshment the haill day, Tibbie was earnest wi' him to take a bite of meat, but he couldna think o't, nor would he take his foot out of the stirrup, and took off the brandy wholly at twa draughts, and named a toast at each. The first was, the memory of Sir Robert Redgauntlet, and might he never lie quiet in his grave till he had righted his poor bond-tenant ; and the second was, a health to Man's Enemy, if he would but get him back the pock of siller, or tell him what came o't, for he saw the haill world was like to regard him as a thief and a cheat, and he took that waur than even the ruin of his house and hauld.

On he rode, little caring where. It was a dark night turned, and the trees made it yet darker, and he let the beast take its ain road through the wood ; when, all of a sudden, from tired and wearied that it was before, the nag began to spring, and flee, and stend, that my gudesire could hardly keep the saddle. Upon the whilk, a horseman, suddenly riding up beside him, said, "That's a mettle beast of yours, freend ; will you sell him?" So saying, he touched the horse's neck with his riding-wand, and it fell into its auld heigh-ho of a stumbling trot. "But his spunk's soon out of him, I think," continued the stranger, "and that is like mony a man's courage, that thinks he wad do great things till he come to the proof."

My gudesire scarce listened to this, but spurred his horse, with "Gude e'en to you, freend."

But it's like the stranger was ane that doesna lightly yield his point; for, ride as Steenie liked, he was aye beside him at the self-same pace. At last my gudesire, Steenie Steenson, grew half angry; and, to say the truth, half feared.

"What is it that ye want with me, freend?" he said. "If ye be a robber, I have nae money; if ye be a leal man, wanting company, I have nae heart to mirth or speaking; and if ye want to ken the road, I scarce ken it mysell."

"If you will tell me your grief," said the stranger, "I am one that, though I have been sair miscaa'd in the world, am the only hand for helping my freends."

So my gudesire, to ease his ain heart, mair than from any hope of help, told him the story from beginning to end.

"It's a hard pinch," said the stranger; "but I think I can help you."

"If you could lend the money, sir, and take a lang day—I ken nae other help on earth," said my gudesire.

"But there may be some under the earth," said the stranger. "Come, I'll be frank wi' you; I could lend you the money on bond, but you would maybe scruple my terms. Now, I can tell you, that your auld Laird is disturbed in his grave by your curses, and the wailing of your family, and if ye daur venture to go to see him, he will give you the receipt."

My gudesire's hair stood on end at this proposal, but he thought his companion might be some humorsome chield that was trying to frighten him, and might end with lending him the money. Besides, he was bauld wi' brandy, and desperate wi' distress ; and he said he had courage to go to the gate of hell, and a step farther, for that receipt. The stranger laughed.

Weel, they rode on through the thickest of the wood, when, all of a sudden, the horse stopped at the door of a great house ; and, but that he knew the place was ten miles off, my father would have thought he was at Redgauntlet Castle. They rode into the outer courtyard, through the muckle faulding yetts, and aneath the auld portcullis ; and the whole front of the house was lighted, and there were pipes and fiddles, and as much dancing and deray within as used to be in Sir Robert's house at Pace and Yule, and such high seasons. They lap off, and my gudesire, as seemed to him, fastened his horse to the very ring he had tied him to that morning, when he gaed to wait on the young Sir John.

" God ! " said my gudesire, " if Sir Robert's death be but a dream ! "

He knocked at the ha' door just as he was wont, and his auld acquaintance, Dougal MacCallum—just after his wont, too—came to open the door, and said, " Piper Steenie, are ye there, lad ? Sir Robert has been crying for you."

My gudesire was like a man in a dream—he looked for the stranger, but he was gane for the time. At last he just tried to say, " Ha ! Dougal Driveower, are ye living ? I thought ye had been dead."

" Never fash yoursell wi' me," said Dougal, " but look to yoursell ; and see ye tak naething frae onybody here, neither meat, drink, or siller, except just the receipt that is your ain."

So saying, he led the way out through halls and

trances that were weel kend to my gudesire, and into the auld oak parlour ; and there was as much singing of profane sangs, and birling of red wine, and speaking blasphemy and sculduddry, as had ever been in Redgauntlet Castle when it was at the blithest.

But, Lord take us in keeping ! what a set of ghastly revellers they were that sat round that table ! My gudesire kend mony that had long before gane to their place, for often had he piped to the most part in the hall of Redgauntlet. There was the fierce Middleton, and the dissolute Rothes, and the crafty Lauderdale ; and Dalyell, with his bald head and a beard to his girdle ; and Earlshall, with Cameron's blude on his hand ; and wild Bonshaw, that tied blessed Mr. Cargill's limbs till the blude sprang ; and Dumbarton Douglas, the twice-turned traitor baith to country and king. There was the Bluidy Advocate MacKenyie, who, for his worldly wit and wisdom, had been to the rest as a god. And there was Claverhouse, as beautiful as when he lived, with his long, dark, curled locks, streaming down over his laced buff-coat, and his left hand always on his right spule-blade, to hide the wound that the silver bullet had made. He sat apart from them all, and looked at them with a melancholy, haughty countenance ; while the rest hallooed, and sung, and laughed, that the room rang. But their smiles were fearfully contorted from time to time ; and their laughter passed into such wild sounds as made my gudesire's very nails grow blue, and chilled the marrow in his banes.

They that waited at the table were just the wicked serving-men and troopers, that had done their work and cruel bidding on earth. There was the Lang Lad of the Nethertown, that helped to take Argyle ; and the Bishop's summoner, that they called the Deil's

Rattle-bag ; and the wicked guardsmen, in their laced coats ; and the savage Highland Amorites, that shed blood like water ; and many a proud serving-man, haughty of heart and bloody of hand, cringing to the rich, and making them wickeder than they would be ; grinding the poor to powder, when the rich had broken them to fragments. And mony, mony mair were coming and ganging, a' as busy in their vocation as if they had been alive.

Sir Robert Redgauntlet, in the midst of a' this fearful riot, cried, wi' a voice like thunder, on Steenie Piper, to come to the board-head where he was sitting ; his legs stretched out before him, and swathed up with flannel, with his holster pistols aside him, while the great broadsword rested against his chair, just as my gudesire had seen him the last time upon earth—the very cushion for the jackanape was close to him, but the creature itsell was not there—it wasna its hour, it's likely ; for he heard them say as he came forward, " Is not the Major come yet ? " And another answered, " The jackanape will be here betimes the morn." And when my gudesire came forward, Sir Robert, or his ghaist, or the deevil in his likeness, said, " Weel, piper, hae ye settled wi' my son for the year's rent ? "

With much ado my gudesire gat breath to say that Sir John would not settle without his honour's receipt.

" Ye shall hae that for a tune of the pipes, Steenie," said the appearance of Sir Robert. " Play us up ' Weel hoddled, Luckie.' "

Now this was a tune my gudesire learned frae a warlock, that heard it when they were worshipping Satan at their meetings ; and my gudesire had sometimes played it at the ranting suppers in Redgauntlet Castle, but never very willingly ; and now he grew cauld at the very name of it, and said, for excuse, he hadna his pipes wi' him.

" MacCallum, ye limb of Beelzebub," said the fearfu' Sir Robert, " bring Steenie the pipes that I am keeping for him ! "

MacCallum brought a pair of pipes that might have served the piper of Donald of the Isles. But he gave my gudesire a nudge as he offered them ; and, looking secretly and closely, Steenie saw that the chanter was of steel and heated to a white heat ; so he had fair warning not to trust his fingers with it. So he excused himself again, and said he was faint and frightened, and had not wind aneugh to fill the bag.

" Then ye maun eat and drink, Steenie," said the figure ; " for we do little else here ; and it's ill speaking between a fou man and a fasting."

Now these were the very words that the bloody Earl of Douglas said to keep the King's messenger in hand while he cut the head off MacLellan of Bombie, at the Threave Castle ; and that put Steenie mair and mair on his guard. So he spoke up like a man, and said he came neither to eat, nor drink, nor make minstrelsy ; but simply for his ain—to ken what was come o' the money he had paid, and to get a discharge for it ; and he was so stout-hearted by this time that he charged Sir Robert for conscience' sake—(he had no power to say the holy name)—and, as he hoped for peace and rest, to spread no snares for him, but just to give him his ain.

The appearance gnashed its teeth and laughed, but it took from a large pocket-book the receipt, and handed it to Steenie. " There is your receipt, ye pitiful cur ; and for the money, my dog-whelp of a son may go look for it in the Cat's Cradle."

My gudesire uttered mony thanks, and was about to retire when Sir Robert roared aloud, " Stop, though, thou sack-doudling son of a whore! I am not done with thee. HERE we do nothing for nothing; and you must return on this very day twelvemonth, to pay your master the homage that you owe me for my protection."

My gudesire's tongue was loosed of a suddenty, and he said aloud, "I refer mysell to God's pleasure, and not to yours."

He had no sooner uttered the word than all was dark around him; and he sunk on the earth with such a sudden shock that he lost both breath and sense.

How lang Steenie lay there, he could not tell; but when he came to himsell, he was lying in the auld kirkyard of Redgauntlet parochine just at the door of the family aisle, and the scutcheon of the auld knight, Sir Robert, hanging over his head. There was a deep morning fog on grass and gravestane around him, and his horse was feeding quietly beside the minister's twa cows. Steenie would have thought the whole was a dream, but he had the receipt in his hand, fairly written and signed by the auld Laird; only the last letters of his name were a little disorderly, written like one seized with sudden pain.

Sorely troubled in his mind, he left that dreary place, rode through the mist to Redgauntlet Castle, and with much ado he got speech of the Laird.

"Well, you dyvour bankrupt," was the first word, "have you brought me my rent?"

"No," answered my gudesire, "I have not; but I have brought your honour Sir Robert's receipt for it."

"How, sirrah? Sir Robert's receipt! You told me he had not given you one."

"Will your honour please see if that bit line is right?"

Sir John looked at every line, and at every letter,

with much attention ; and at last, at the date, which my gudesire had not observed. " *From my appointed place,*" he read, " *this twenty-fifth of November.*" " What ! That is yesterday ! Villain, thou must have gone to hell for this ! "

" I got it from your honour's father—whether he be in heaven or hell, I know not," said Steenie.

" I will delate you for a warlock to the Privy Council ! " said Sir John. " I will send you to your master, the devil, with the help of a tar-barrel and a torch ! "

" I intend to delate mysell to the Presbytery," said Steenie, " and tell them all I have seen last night, whilk are things fitter for them to judge of than a borrel man like me."

Sir John paused, composed himsell, and desired to hear the full history ; and my gudesire told it him from point to point, as I have told it you—word for word, neither more nor less.

Sir John was silent again for a long time, and at last he said, very composedly, " Steenie, this story of yours concerns the honour of many a noble family besides mine ; and if it be a leasing-making, to keep yourself out of my danger, the least you can expect is to have a red-hot iron driven through your tongue, and that will be as bad as scauding your fingers with a red-hot chanter. But yet it may be true, Steenie ; and if the money cast up, I shall not know what to think of it. But where shall we find the Cat's Cradle ? There are cats enough about the old house, but I think they kitten without the ceremony of bed or cradle."

" We were best ask Hutcheon," said my gudesire ; " he kens a' the odd corners about as weel as—another serving-man that is now gane, and that I wad not like to name."

Aweel, Hutcheon, when he was asked, told them, that a ruinous turret, lang disused, next to the clock-house, only accessible by a ladder, for the opening was on the outside, and far above the battlements, was called of old the Cat's Cradle.

'There will I go immediately," said Sir John, and he took (with what purpose, Heaven kens) one of his father's pistols from the hall-table, where they had lain since the night he died, and hastened to the battlements.

It was a dangerous place to climb, for the ladder was auld and frail, and wanted ane or twa rounds. However, up got Sir John, and entered at the turret door, where his body stopped the only little light that was in the bit turret. Something flees at him wi' a vengeance, maist dang him back ower—bang gaed the knight's pistol, and Hutcheon, that held the ladder, and my gudesire that stood beside him, hears a loud skelloch. A minute after, Sir John flings the body of the jackanape down to them, and cries that the siller is fund, and that they should come up and help him. And there was the bag of siller sure aneugh, and mony orra things besides, that had been missing for mony a day. And Sir John, when he had riped the turret weel, led my gudesire into the dining-parlour, and took him by the hand, and spoke kindly to him, and said he was sorry he should have doubted his word, and that he would hereafter be a good master to him, to make amends.

" And now, Steenie," said Sir John, " although this vision of yours tends, on the whole, to my father's credit, as an honest man, that he should, even after his death, desire to see justice done to a poor man like you, yet you are sensible that ill-dispositioned men might make bad constructions upon it, concerning his soul's health. So, I think, we had better lay the haill dirdum on that ill-deedie creature, Major Weir, and say naething about your dream in the wood of Pitmurkie. You had taken ower muckle brandy to be very certain about onything; and, Steenie, this receipt" (his hand shook while he held it out)—"it's but a queer kind of document, and we will do best, I think, to put it quietly in the fire."

"Od, but for as queer as it is, it's a' the voucher I have for my rent," said my gudesire, who was afraid, it may be, of losing the benefit of Sir Robert's discharge.

"I will bear the contents to your credit in the rental-book, and give you a discharge under my own hand," said Sir John, "and that on the spot. And, Steenie, if you can hold your tongue about this matter, you shall sit, from this term downward, at an easier rent."

"Mony thanks to your honour," said Steenie, who saw easily in what corner the wind was; "doubtless I will be comfortable to all your honour's commands; only I would willingly speak wi' some powerful minister on the subject, for I do not like the sort of soumons of appointment whilk your honour's father——"

"Do not call the phantom my father!" said Sir John, interrupting him.

"Weel, then, the thing that was so like him," said my gudesire; "he spoke of my coming back to him this time twelvemonth, and it's a weight on my conscience."

"Aweel, then," said Sir John, "if you be so much distressed in mind, you may speak to our minister of the parish; he is a douce man, regards the honour of our family, and the mair that he may look for some patronage from me."

Wi' that, my gudesire readily agreed that the receipt should be burnt, and the Laird threw it into the chimney with his ain hand. Burn it would not for them, though ; but away it flew up the lum, wi' a lang train of sparks at its tail, and a hissing noise like a squib.

My gudesire gaed down to the manse, and the minister, when he had heard the story, said it was his real opinion that though my gudesire had gaen very far in tampering with dangerous matters, yet, as he had refused the devil's arles (for such was the offer of meat and drink), and had refused to do homage by piping at his bidding, he hoped that, if he held a circumspect walk hereafter, Satan could take little advantage by what was come and gane. And, indeed, my gudesire, of his ain accord, long forswore baith the pipes and the brandy—it was not even till the year was out, and the fatal day passed, that he would so much as take the fiddle, or drink usquebaugh or tippenny.

Sir John made up his story about the jackanape as he liked himsell ; and some believe to this day there was no more in the matter than the filching nature of the brute. Indeed, ye'll no hinder some to threap that it was nane o' the Auld Enemy that Dougal and Hutcheon saw in the Laird's room, but only that wanchancy creature, the Major, capering on the coffin ; and that, as to the blawing on the Laird's whistle that was heard after he was dead, the filthy brute could do that as weel as the Laird himsell, if no better. But Heaven kens the truth, whilk first came out by the minister's wife, after Sir John and her ain gudeman were baith in the moulds. And then my gudesire, wha was failed in his limbs, but not in his judgment or memory—at least nothing to speak of—was obliged to tell the real narrative to his freends, for the credit of his good name. He might else have been charged for a warlock.

SIR WALTER SCOTT. (From *Redgauntlet.*)

THE TALE OF TOD LAPRAIK

MY faither, Tam Dale, peace to his banes, was a wild, sploring lad in his young days, wi' little wisdom and little grace. He was fond of a lass and fond of a glass, and fond of a ran-dan ; but I could never hear tell that he was muckle use for honest employment. Frae ae thing to anither, he listed at last for a sodger and was in the garrison of this fort, which was the first way that ony of the Dales cam to set foot upon the Bass. Sorrow upon that service ! The governor brewed his ain ale ; it seems it was the warst conceivable. The rock was proveesioned frae the shores with vivers, the thing was ill-guided, and there were whiles when they but to fish and shoot solans for their diet. To crown a', thir was the Days of the Persecution. The perishin' cauld chalmers were all occupied wi' sants and martyrs, the saut of the yearth, of which it wasnae worthy. And though Tam Dale carried a firelock there, a single sodger, and he liked a lass and a glass, as I was sayin', the mind of the man was mair just than set with his position. He had glints of the glory of the kirk ; there were whiles when his dander rase to see the Lord's sants misguided, and shame covered him that he should be haulding a canl'e (or carrying a firelock) in so black a business. There were nights of it when he was here on sentry, the place a' wheesht, the frosts o' winter maybe riving in the wa's, and he would hear ane o' the prisoners strike up a psalm, and the rest join in, and the blessed sounds rising from the different chalmers—or dungeons, I would raither say —so that this auld craig in the sea was like a pairt of Heev'n. Black shame was on his saul ; his sins hove up before him muckle as the Bass, and above a', that chief sin, that he should have a hand in hagging and hashing at Christ's Kirk. But the truth is that he resisted the spirit. Day cam, there were the rousing compainions, and his guid resolves depairtit.

In thir days, dwalled upon the Bass a man of God, Peden the Prophet was his name. Ye'll have heard tell of Prophet Peden. There was never the wale of him sinsyne, and it's a question wi' mony if there ever was his like afore. He was wild 's a peat-hag, fearsome to look at, fearsome to hear, his face like the day of judgment. The voice of him was like a solan's and dinnle'd in folks' lugs, and the words of him like coals of fire.

Now there was a lass on the rock, and I think she had little to do, for it was nae place far dacent weemen ; but it seems she was bonny, and her and Tam Dale were very well agreed. It befell that Peden was in the gairden his lane at the praying when Tam and the lass cam by ; and what should the lassie do but mock with laughter at the sant's devotions ? He rose and lookit at the twa o' them, and Tam's knees knoitered thegether at the look of him. But whan he spak, it was mair in sorrow than in anger. " Poor thing, poor thing ! " says he, and it was the lass he lookit at, " I hear you skirl and laugh," he says, " but the Lord has a deid shot prepared for you, and at that surprising judgment ye shall skirl but the ae time ! " Shortly thereafter she was daundering on the craigs wi' twa-three sodgers, and it was a blawy day. There cam a gowst of wind, claught her by the coats, and awa' wi' her bag and baggage. And it was remarked by the sodgers that she gied but the ae skirl.

Nae doubt this judgment had some weicht upon Tam Dale ; but it passed again and him none the better.

Ae day he was flyting wi' anither sodger-lad. " Deil hae me ! " quo' Tam, for he was a profane swearer. And there was Peden glowering at him, gash an' waefu' ; Peden wi' his lang chafts an' luntin' een, the maud happed about his kist, and the hand of him held out wi' the black nails upon the finger-nebs—for he had nae care of the body. " Fy, fy, poor man ! " cries he, " the poor fool man ! *Deil hae me*, quo' he ; an' I see the deil at his oxter." The conviction of guilt and grace cam in on Tam like the deep sea ; he flang doun the pike that was in his hands—" I will nae mair lift arms against the cause o' Christ ! " says he, and was as gude's word. There was a sair fyke in the beginning, but the governor seeing him resolved, gied him his dischairge, and he went and dwallt and merried in North Berwick, and had aye a gude name with honest folk frae that day on.

It was in the year seeventeen hunner and sax that the Bass cam in the hands o' the Da'rymples, and there was twa men soucht the chairge of it. Baith were weel qualified, for they had baith been sodgers in the garrison, and kent the gate to handle solans, and the seasons and values of them. Forby that they were baith—or they baith seemed—earnest professors and men of comely conversation. The first of them was just Tam Dale, my faither. The second was ane Lapraik, whom the folk ca'd Tod Lapraik maistly, but whether for his name or his nature I could never hear tell. Weel, Tam gaed to see Lapraik upon this business, and took me, that was a toddlin' laddie, by the hand. Tod had his dwallin' in the lang loan benorth the kirk-yaird. It's a dark uncanny loan, forby that the kirk has aye had an ill name since the days o' James the Saxt and the deevil's cantrips played therein when the Queen was on the seas ; and as for Tod's house, it was in the mirkiest end, and was little liked by some that kenned the best. The door was on the sneck that day, and me and my faither gaed straucht in. Tod was a wabster to his trade ; his loom stood in the but. There he sat, a muckle fat, white hash of a man like creish, wi' a kind of a holy smile that gart me scunner. The hand of him aye cawed the shuttle, but his een was steeked. We cried to him by his name, we skirled in the deid lug of him, we shook him by the shou'ther. Nae mainner o' service ! There he sat on his dowp, an' cawed the shuttle and smiled like creish.

" God be guid to us," says Tam Dale, " this is no canny."

He had jimp said the word, when Tod Lapraik cam to himsel'.

" Is this you, Tam ? " says he. " Haith, man ! I'm blithe to see ye. I whiles fa' into a bit dwam like this," he says ; " it's frae the stamach."

Weel, they began to crack about the Bass and which of them twa was to get the warding o't, and little by little cam to very ill words, and twined in anger. I mind weel that as my faither and me gaed hame again, he cam ower and ower the same expression, how little he likit Tod Lapraik and his dwams.

" Dwam ! " says he. " I think folk hae brunt for dwams like yon."

Aweel, my faither got the Bass and Tod had to go wantin'. It was remembered sinsyne what way he had ta'en the thing. " Tam," says he, " ye hae gotten the better o' me aince mair, and I hope," says he, " ye'll find at least a' that ye expeckit at the Bass." Which have since been thought remarkable expressions. At last the time came for Tam Dale to take young solans. This was a business he was weel used wi', he had been a craigsman frae a laddie, and trustit nane but himsel'. So there was he hingin' by a line an' speldering on the craig face, whaur it's hieest and steighest. Fower tenty lads were on the tap, hauldin' the line and mindin' for his signals. But whaur Tam hung there was naething but the craig, and the sea belaw, and the solan's skirlin' and flying. It was a braw spring morn, and Tam whustled as he claught in the young geese. Mony's the time I've heard him tell of this experience, and aye the swat ran upon the man.

It chanced, ye see, that Tam keeked up, and he was awaur of a muckle solan, and the solan pyking at the line. He thocht this by-ordinar and outside the creature's habits. He minded that ropes were unco saft things and the solan's neb and the Bass Rock unco hard, and that twa hunner feet were raither mair than he would care to fa'.

" Shoo ! " says Tam. " Awa', bird ! Shoo, awa' wi' ye ! " says he.

The solan keekit doon into Tam's face, and there was something unco in the creature's ee. Just the ae keek it gied, and back to the rope. But now it wroucht and warstl't like a thing dementit. There never was the solan made that wroucht as that solan wroucht ; and it seemed to understand its employ brawly, birzing the saft rope between the neb of it and a crunkled jag o' stane.

There gaed a cauld stend o' fear into Tam's heart. " This thing is nae bird," thinks he. His een turnt backward in his heid and the day gaed black aboot him. " If I get a dwam here," he thoucht, " it's by wi' Tam Dale." And he signalled for the lads to pu' him up.

And it seemed the solan understood about signals. For nae sooner was the signal made than he let be the rope, spried his wings, squawked out loud, took a turn flying, and dashed straucht at Tam Dale's een. Tam had a knife, he gart the cauld steel glitter. And it seemed the solan understood about knives, for nae suner did the steel glint in the sun than he gied the ae squawk, but laigher, like a body disappointit, and flegged aff about the roundness of the craig, and Tam saw him nae mair. And as sune as that thing was gane, Tam's heid drapt upon his shouther, and they pu'd him up like a deid corp, dadding on the craig.

A dram of brandy (which he went never without) broucht him to his mind, or what was left of it. Up he sat.

" Rin, Geordie, rin to the boat, mak' sure of the boat, man—rin ! " he cries, " or yon solan'll have it awa'," says he.

The fower lads stared at ither, an' tried to whilly-wha him to be quiet. But naething would satisfy Tam Dale, till ane o' them had startit on aheid to stand sentry on the boat. The ithers askit if he was for down again.

" Na," says he, " and neither you nor me," says he, " and as sune as I can win to stand on my twa feet we'll be aff this craig o' Sawtan."

Sure eneuch, nae time was lost, and that was ower muckle ; for before they won to North Berwick Tam was in a crying fever. He lay a' the simmer ; and wha was sae kind as come speiring for him, but Tod Lapraik ! Folk thocht afterwards that ilka time Tod cam near the house the fever had worsened. I kenna for that ; but what I ken the best, that was the end of it.

It was about this time o' the year ; my grandfaither was out at the white fishing ; and like a bairn, I but to gang wi' him. We had a grand take, I mind, and the way that the fish lay broucht us near in by the Bass, whaur we foregaithered wi' another boat that belanged to a man Sandie Fletcher in Castleton. He's no lang deid neither, or ye could speir at himsel'. Weel, Sandie hailed.

" What's yon on the Bass ? " says he.

" On the Bass ? " says grandfaither.

" Ay," says Sandie, " on the green side o't."

" Whatten kind of a thing ? " says grandfaither. " There cannae be naething on the Bass but just the sheep."

" It looks unco like a body," quo' Sandie, who was nearer in.

" A body ! " says we, and we none of us likit that. For there was nae boat that could have brought a man, and the key o' the prison yett hung ower my faither's heid at hame in the press bed.

We keept the twa boats closs for company, and crap in nearer hand. Grandfaither had a gless, for he had been a sailor, and the captain of a smack, and had lost her on the sands of Tay. And when we took the gless to it, sure eneuch there was a man. He was in a crunkle o' green brae, a wee below the chaipel, a' by his lee lane, and lowped and flang and danced like a daft quean at a waddin'.

" It's Tod," says grandfaither, and passed the gless to Sandie.

" Ay, it's him," says Sandie.

" Or ane in the likeness o' him," says grandfaither.

" Sma' is the differ," quo' Sandie. " Deil or warlock, I'll try the gun at him," quo' he, and broucht up a fowling-piece that he aye carried, for Sandie was a notable famous shot in all that country.

" Haud your hand, Sandie," says grandfaither ;

" we maun see clearer first," says he, " or this may be a dear day's wark to the baith of us."

" Hout ! " says Sandie, " this is the Lord's judgment surely, and be damned to it," says he.

" Maybe ay, and maybe no," says my grandfaither, worthy man ! " But have you a mind of the Procurator Fiscal, that I think ye'll have foregaithered wi' before," says he.

This was ower true, and Sandie was a wee thing set ajee. " Aweel, Edie," says he, " and what would be your way of it ? "

" Ou, just this," says grandfaither. " Let me that has the fastest boat gang back to North Berwick, and let you bide here and keep an eye on Thon. If I cannae find Lapraik, I'll join ye and the twa of us'll have a crack wi' him. But if Lapraik's at hame, I'll rin up the flag at the harbour, and ye can try Thon Thing wi' the gun."

Aweel, so it was agreed between them twa. I was just a bairn, an' clum in Sandie's boat, whaur I thoucht I would see the best of the employ. My grandsire gied Sandie a siller tester to pit in his gun wi' the leid draps, bein mair deidly again bogles. And then the ae boat set aff for North Berwick, an' the tither lay whaur it was and watched the wanchancy thing on the braeside.

A' the time we lay there it lowped and flang and capered and span like a teetotum, and whiles we could hear it skelloch as it span. I hae seen lassies, the daft queans, that would lowp and dance a winter's nicht, and still be lowping and dancing when the winter's day cam in. But there would be fowk there to hauld them company, and the lads to egg them on ; and this thing was its lee-lane. And there would be a fiddler diddling his elbock in the chimney-side ; and this thing had nae music but the skirling of the solans. And the lassies were bits o' young things wi' the reid life dinnling and stending in their members ; and this was a muckle, fat, creishy man, and him fa'n in the vale o' years. Say what ye like, I maun say what I believe. It was joy was in the creature's heart, the joy o' hell, I daursay : joy whatever. Mony a time I have askit mysel' why witches and warlocks should sell their sauls (whilk are their maist dear possessions) and be auld, duddy, wrunkl't wives or auld, feckless, doddered men ; and then I mind upon Tod Lapraik dancing a' the hours by his lane in the black glory of his heart. Nae doubt they burn for it muckle in hell, but they have a grand time here of it, whatever !—and the Lord forgie us !

Weel, at the hinder end, we saw the wee flag yirk up to the mast-heid upon the harbour rocks. That was a' Sandie waited for. He up wi' the gun, took a deleeberate aim, an' pu'd the trigger. There cam' a bang and then ae waefu' skirl frae the Bass. And there were we rubbin' our een and lookin' at ither like daft folk. For wi' the bang and the skirl the thing had clean disappeared. The sun glintit, the wind blew, and there was the bare yaird whaur the Wonder had been lowping and flinging but ae second syne.

The hale way hame I roared and grat wi' the terror o' that dispensation. The grawn folk were nane sae muckle better ; there was little said in Sandie's boat but just the name of God ; and when we won in by the pier, the harbour rocks were fair black wi' the folk waitin' us. It seems they had fund Lapraik in ane of his dwams, cawing the shuttle and smiling. Ae lad they sent to hoist the flag, and the rest abode there in the wabster's house. You may be sure they liked it little ; but it was a means of grace to severals that stood there praying in to themsel's (for nane cared to pray out loud) and looking on thon awesome thing as it cawed the shuttle. Syne, upon a suddenty, and wi' the ae dreidfu' skelloch, Tod sprang up frae his hinderlands and fell forrit on the wab, a bluidy corp.

When the corp was examined the leid draps hadnae played buff upon the warlock's body; sorrow a leid drap was to be fund! but there was grandfaither's siller tester in the puddock's heart of him.

ROBERT LOUIS STEVENSON.
(From *Catriona.*)

GLOSSARY (to Pages 19–51)

a', all
ae, one
ain, own
ajee, awry
anes and aye, once and always
arles, earnest-money
auld, old
awa', away
aweel, well
ay, yes
aye, ever, always

bartizan, battlement
bide, stay
birling, drinking
birzing, bruising
blaud, few verses
borrel, unlettered
brash, storm
braw, fine
brunt, burned
but, (1) had, (2) outer room

ca' caa'd, call, called
caller, bracing
cankered, ill-humoured
canny, of good omen
cantrips, tricks
carle, fellow
caw, drive
chafts, jaws, cheeks
chape, metal mounting of scabbard
cheild, chiel, fellow
claught, clutched
closs, close
coats, petticoats
cowped, upset
crack, talk
crap, crept
creish, grease
crunkle, wrinkle

dadding, knocking
dang, knocked
dargle, dell
daundering, sauntering
daur, dare
deid, dead
deil, devil
delate, accuse
deray, noise of banqueting
diddling, jogging
dinnle'd, rattled
dirdum, blame
doddered, decayed
douce, sedate
dowp, buttocks
duddy, ragged
dwam, swoon
dyvour, good for nothing

een, eyes
elbock, elbow

fa', fa'n, fall, fallen
fand, found
fash, fasherie, trouble
faur'd, favoured

feckless, feeble
flegged, fluttered
flyting, brawling
forby, besides
fou, full
fower, four
fowk, folk
frae, from
fyke, fuss

gae, gave
gang, gaed, go, went
gar, gart, garred, make, made
gash, solemn
gate, way
gied, gave
girned, snarled
glints, glimpses
grat, wept
grit oath, Bible oath
grue, shudder
gudesire, grandfather
guid, good

ha', hall
hagging, hacking
haill, hale, whole
haith, faith
happed, wrapped
hash, mess
hashing, slashing
hauld, (1) hold, (2) holding
hesp, hank of yarn
hoddled, waddled
hove, rose
howlets, owls

ill-deedie, mischievous
ilka, every
ither, other, each other

jackanape, monkey
jimp, scarcely

keek, look
ken, kenned, kent, know, knew
kenna, know not
kist, chest
knoitered, knocked

laigher, lower
laith, unwilling
lane, lain, lee-lane, alone
leal, faithful
leasing-making, calumniating
leid, lead
loan, road
lug, ear
lum, chimney
lunting, blazing

mails, rents
mair, more
maud, cloak
maun, must
mear, mare
merk, 13/4d. Scots=1/1⅓d. English
mirkest, darkest
mony, many
muckle, much
muils, slippers

nane, none
neb, nose
neist, next

orra, miscellaneous
orra sough, occasional rumour
ower, over
oxter, armpit

Pace, Easter
parochine, parish
pock, bag
Procurator Fiscal, the public prosecutor for the county
press-bed, box-bed
pu', pull
puddock, frog
pyking, picking

quean, wench

rattle-bag, noisy person
rattling, rollicking
rase, rose
riped, ransacked
riving, raging, tearing
round, turret
rug, tear (share of the spoil)

sack-doudling, droning on the bag-pipes
saut, salt
scowp, run off
sculduddery, lewd
scunner, disgust
siller, silver, money
sinsyne, since, afterwards
skelloch, yell
skirl, scream
sleekit, insinuating
sneck, latch
solan, a solan goose
soumons, summons
speerings, speiring, news, inquiry
speldering, sprawling
sploring, roistering
spried, spread
spule, shoulder

spunk, spirit
steeked, shut
steighest, steepest
stend, leap
syne, then, since

tangs, tongs
tass, goblet
tenty, attentive, watchful
thir, these, those
threap, persist
tippenny, ale, small beer
tither, other
tod, fox
toom, empty
trances, passages
twa, two
twined, parted

unco, uncommonly
usquebaugh, whisky

vivers, food

wab, web
wabster, weaver
wale, equal
wame, belly
wanchancy, unlucky
wared, expended
warlock, wizard
warstl't, wrestled
wa's, walls
waur, worse
wheesht, hushed
whiles, sometimes
whilk, which
whilly-wa, coax
wuss, wish

yelloch, yell
yett, gate
yirk, jerk

TAM O' SHANTER

WHEN chapman billies leave the street,   pedlar fellows
And drouthy neebors, neebors meet,   thirsty
As market-days are wearing late,
An' folk begin to tak the gate ;   road
While we sit bousing at the nappy,   ale
An' getting fou and unco happy,   drunk ; very
We think na on the lang Scots miles,   not
The mosses, waters, slaps, and styles,   gaps in walls
That lie between us and our hame,
Whare sits our sulky sullen dame,
Gathering her brows like gathering storm,
Nursing her wrath to keep it warm.

This truth fand honest Tam o' Shanter,   found
As he frae Ayr ae night did canter,
(Auld Ayr, wham ne'er a town surpasses,
For honest men and bonny lasses.)

O Tam! hads't thou but been sae wise,
As ta'en thy ain wife Kate's advice!
good-for-nothing — She tauld thee weel thou was a skellum,
chattering; babbler — A blethering, blustering, drunken blellum;
That frae November till October,
Ae market-day thou was na sober
at every meal-grinding — That ilka melder, wi' the miller,
money — Thou sat as long as thou had siller;
nag that had a shoe put on — That ev'ry naig was ca'd a shoe on,
The smith and thee gat roaring fou on;
That at the Lord's house, even on Sunday,
Thou drank wi' Kirkton Jean till Monday.
She prophesied that, late or soon,
Thou would be found deep drown'd in
    Doon;
wizards; dark — Or catch'd wi' warlocks in the mirk,
By Alloway's auld haunted kirk.

makes; weep — Ah, gentle dames! it gars me greet,
To think how mony counsels sweet,
How mony lengthen'd sage advices,
The husband frae the wife despises!

But to our tale:—Ae market-night,
Tam had got planted unco right;
Fast by an ingle, bleezing finely,
foaming ale — Wi' reaming swats, that drank divinely;
cobbler — And at his elbow, Souter Johnny,
His ancient, trusty, drouthy crony;
Tam lo'ed him like a vera brither;
They had been fou for weeks thegither.
The night drave on wi' sangs and clatter;
And aye the ale was growing better:
The landlady and Tam grew gracious,
Wi' favours secret, sweet, and precious:

The Souter tauld his queerest stories;
The landlord's laugh was ready chorus:
The storm without might rair and rustle, roar
Tam did na mind the storm a whistle.

Care, mad to see a man sae happy,
E'en drown'd himsel amang the nappy!
As bees flee hame wi' lades o' treasure, loads
The minutes wing'd their way wi' pleasure:
Kings may be blest, but Tam was glorious,
O'er a' the ills o' life victorious!

But pleasures are like poppies spread,
You seize the flow'r, its bloom is shed;
Or like the snowfall in the river,
A moment white—then melts for ever;
Or like the borealis race,
That flit ere you can point their place;
Or like the rainbow's lovely form
Evanishing amid the storm.—
Nae man can tether time or tide;
The hour approaches Tam maun ride;
That hour, o' night's black arch the key-stane,
That dreary hour he mounts his beast in;
And sic a night he taks the road in,
As ne'er poor sinner was abroad in.

The wind blew as 'twad blawn its last; would have
The rattling showers rose on the blast;
The speedy gleams the darkness swallow'd;
Loud, deep, and lang, the thunder bellow'd:
That night, a child might understand,
The Deil had business on his hand.

Weel mounted on his grey mare, Meg—
A better never lifted leg—

thrashed ; puddle	Tam skelpit on thro' dub and mire,
	Despising wind, and rain, and fire ;
now	Whiles holding fast his gude blue bonnet ;
	Whiles crooning o'er some auld Scots sonnet ;
staring	Whiles glow'ring round wi' prudent cares,
	Lest bogles catch him unawares :
	Kirk-Alloway was drawing nigh,
owls	Whare ghaists and houlets nightly cry.
	By this time he was cross the ford,
smothered	Whare in the snaw the chapman smoor'd ;
birches ; big	And past the birks and meikle stane,
	Whare drunken Charlie brak's neck-bane ;
furze	And thro' the whins, and by the cairn,
	Whare hunters fand the murder'd bairn ;
above	And near the thorn, aboon the well,
	Whare Mungo's mither hang'd hersel'.
	Before him Doon pours all his floods ;
	The doubling storm roars thro' the woods ;
	The lightnings flash from pole to pole ;
	Near and more near the thunders roll :
	When, glimmering thro' the groaning trees,
	Kirk-Alloway seem'd in a bleeze ;
every chink	Thro' ilka bore the beams were glancing ;
	And loud resounded mirth and dancing.
	Inspiring bold John Barleycorn !
	What dangers thou canst make us scorn !
ale	Wi' tippenny, we fear nae evil ;
whisky	Wi' usquabae, we'll face the devil !
	The swats sae ream'd in Tammie's noddle,
not ; farthing	Fair play, he car'd na deils a boddle.
	But Maggie stood right sair astonish'd,
	Till, by the heel and hand admonish'd,

She ventur'd forward on the light;
And, wow! Tam saw an unco sight!   marvellous
Warlocks and witches in a dance;
Nae cotillion, brent new frae France,   brand
But hornpipes, jigs, strathspeys, and reels,
Put life and mettle in their heels.
A winnock-bunker in the east,   window-seat
There sat Auld Nick, in shape o' beast;
A towzie tyke, black, grim, and large,   shaggy dog
To gie them music was his charge:
He screw'd the pipes and gart them skirl,   made ; squeal
Till roof and rafters a' did dirl.   ring
Coffins stood round, like open presses,   cupboards
That shaw'd the dead in their last dresses;
And (by some devilish cantraip sleight)   magic art
Each in its cauld hand held a light:
By which heroic Tam was able
To note upon the haly table,
A murderer's banes in gibbet airns;   irons
Twa span-lang, wee, unchristen'd bairns;
A thief, new-cutted frae a rape—   rope
Wi' his last gasp his gab did gape;   mouth
Five tomahawks, wi' blude red-rusted;
Five scymitars, wi' murder crusted;
A garter, which a babe had strangled;
A knife, a father's throat had mangled,
Whom his ain son o' life bereft,
The grey hairs yet stack to the heft;   stuck ; haft
Wi' mair o' horrible and awefu',
Which even to name wad be unlawfu'.

As Tammie glowr'd, amaz'd, and curious,   stared
The mirth and fun grew fast and furious:
The piper loud and louder blew;
The dancers quick and quicker flew;

clasped hands	They reel'd, they set, they cross'd, they cleekit,
witch ; sweated and steamed	Till ilka carlin swat and reekit,
cast ; rags	And coost her duddies to the wark,
tripped; shift	And linket at it in her sark !
these ; girls	Now, Tam, O Tam ! had thae been queans,
	A' plump and strapping in their teens,
greasy flannel	Their sarks, instead o' creeshie flannen,
	Been snaw-white seventeen hunder linnen !
these	Thir breeks o' mine, my only pair,
	That ance were plush, o' gude blue hair,
buttocks	I wad hae gi'en them off my hurdies,
lasses	For ae blink o' the bonnie burdies !
	But wither'd beldams, auld and droll,
ancient ; wean	Rigwoodie hags wad spean a foal,
leaping ; stick	Lowping and flinging on a crummock,
	I wonder didna turn thy stomach.
knew ; well	But Tam kenn'd what was what fu' brawlie,
choice	There was ae winsome wench and wawlie,
company	That night enlisted in the core,
known	(Lang after kenn'd on Carrick shore ;
	For mony a beast to dead she shot,
	And perish'd mony a bonnie boat,
much ; barley	And shook baith meikle corn and bear,
	And kept the country-side in fear.)
short shift ; cloth	Her cutty sark, o' Paisley harn,
	That while a lassie she had worn,
	In longitude tho' sorely scanty,
proud	It was her best, and she was vauntie.
	Ah ! little kenn'd thy reverend grannie,
bought	That sark she coft for her wee Nannie,
	Wi' twa pund Scots ('twas a' her riches),
	Wad ever grac'd a dance of witches !

But here my Muse her wing maun cour; must stoop
Sic flights are far beyond her pow'r;
To sing how Nannie lap and flang, leaped and kicked
(A souple jade she was, and strang),
And how Tam stood, like ane bewitch'd,
And thought his very een enrich'd;
Even Satan glower'd, and fidg'd fu' fain, fidgeted with delight
And hotch'd and blew wi' might and main: jerked
Till first ae caper, syne anither, then
Tam tint his reason a' thegither, lost
And roars out, "Weel done, Cutty-sark!"
And in an instant all was dark:
And scarcely had he Maggie rallied,
When out the hellish legion sallied.

As bees bizz out wi' angry fyke, fuss
When plundering herds assail their byke; shepherds; hive
As open pussie's mortal foes, the hare's
When, pop! she starts before their nose;
As eager runs the market-crowd,
When "Catch the thief!" resounds aloud;
So Maggie runs, the witches follow,
Wi' mony an eldritch screech and hollow. unearthly; yell

Ah, Tam! Ah, Tam! thou'll get thy fairin'! deserts
In hell they'll roast thee like a herrin'!
In vain thy Kate awaits thy comin'!
Kate soon will be a woefu' woman!
Now, do thy speedy utmost, Meg,
And win the key-stane o' the brig;
There at them thou thy tail may toss,
A running stream they darena cross.
But ere the key-stane she could make,
The fient a tail she had to shake! devil

For Nannie, far before the rest,
Hard upon noble Maggie prest,
intention — And flew at Tam wi' furious ettle;
But little wist she Maggie's mettle—
whole — Ae spring brought off her master hale,
But left behind her ain grey tail:
clutched — The carlin claught her by the rump,
And left poor Maggie scarce a stump.

Now, wha this tale o' truth shall read,
Ilk man and mother's son, take heed:
Whene'er to drink you are inclin'd,
Or cutty-sarks run in your mind,
Think, ye may buy the joys o'er dear—
Remember Tam o' Shanter's mare.

Robert Burns

5. *Bygone Beliefs and Customs*

SHROVE TUESDAY: COCK-FIGHTING

The parish schools of Scotland had their annual saturnalian feast, of what may well be deemed an extraordinary character, if we consider their close connexion with the National Church, and that their teachers were in so many instances licensed clergymen waiting for preferment. On Fasten's eve . . . the schoolmaster, after closing the service of the day with prayer, would call on the boys to divide and choose for themselves "Head-stocks," i.e., leaders, for the yearly cock-fight of the ensuing Shrove-Tuesday. . . .

The grave question of leadership soon settled, in consequence of previous out-of-door arrangement, the master would next proceed to call the boys in alphabetical order ; and each boy to intimate, in reply, under what " head-stock " he proposed fighting his cocks, and how many cocks he intended bringing into the pit. The master, meanwhile, went on recording both items in a book—in especial the number of the cocks—as, according to the registered figure, which always exceeded the array actually brought into the fight, he received, as a fixed perquisite of his office, a fee of twopence per head. The school then broke up ; and for the two ensuing days, which were given as holidays for the purpose of preparation, the parish used to be darkened by wandering scholars going from farmhouse to farmhouse in quest of cocks. . . .

On the morning of Shrove Tuesday, the floor of the school, previously cleared of all the forms, and laid out into a chalked circle representative of the cockpit, became a scene of desperate battle. The master always presided on these occasions as umpire ; while his boys clustered in a ring . . . a little beyond the chalked line. The cocks of the lads who ranged under the one " head-stock " were laid down one after another on the left, those of the other, as a bird dropped exhausted or ran away, upon the right ; and thus the fight went on from morning till far in the evening ; when the " head-stock " whose last bird remained in possession of the field, and whose cocks had routed the greatest number in the aggregate, was declared victor, and formally invested with a tinsel cap, in a ceremony termed the " crowning."

Hugh Miller.

(From *Scenes and Legends of the North af Scotland*, 1834.)

MAY-DAY: BELTANE

On the 1st May the herdmen of each village hold their Beltein, a rural sacrifice. They cut a square trench on the ground, leaving the turf in the middle; on that they make a fire of wood, on which they dress a large caudle of eggs, butter, oatmeal and milk; and bring, besides the ingredients of the caudle, plenty of beer and whisky; for each of the company must contribute something. The rites begin with spilling some of the caudle on the ground, by way of libation: on that, everyone takes a cake of oatmeal, upon which are raised nine square knobs, each dedicated to some particular being, the supposed preserver of their flocks and herds, and to some particular animal, the real destroyer of them. Each person then turns his face to the fire, breaks off a knob, and flinging it over his shoulder, says, "This I give to thee, preserve thou my horses; this to thee, preserve thou my sheep; and so on." After that they use the same ceremony to the noxious animals: "This I give to thee, O fox, spare thou my lambs; this to thee, O hooded crow! this to thee, O eagle!" When the ceremony is over, they dine on the caudle.

Thomas Pennant.

(From *A Tour in Scotland*, 1769.)

Beltane (May 1) and Halloween (October 31), marking the beginnings of summer and winter, were the great fire-festivals of the ancient British Celts. Beltane signifies brightness, and has no connection with the Phœnician Baal.

HALLOWEEN

I

Upon that night, when Fairies light,
  On Cassilis Downans dance,
Or owre the lays, in splendid blaze, leas
  On sprightly coursers prance;
Or for Colean the rout is taen, road
  Beneath the moon's pale beams;
There, up the Cove, to stray an' rove,
  Amang the rocks an' streams
      To sport that night.

II

Amang the bonnie, winding banks,
  Where Doon rins, wimplin', clear, winding
Where Bruce ance rul'd the martial ranks, once
  An' shook his Carrick spear,
Some merry, friendly, countra folks country
  Together did convene,
To burn their nits, an' pou their stocks, nuts; kail plants
  An' haud their Halloween
      Fu' blythe that night.

III

The lasses feat, an' cleanly neat, spruce
  Mair braw than when they're fine;
Their faces blythe fu' sweetly kythe show
  Hearts leal, an' warm, an' kin':
The lads sae trig, wi' wooer-babs, love-knots
  Weel knotted on their garten, garters
Some unco blate, an' some wi' gabs, shy; chatter
  Gar lasses hearts gang startin'
      Whyles fast at night.

IV

	Then, first an' foremost, thro' the kail,
	Their stocks maun a' be sought ance;
shut their eyes; grope;	They steek their een, an' grape an' wale,
choose	
straight	For muckle anes, an' straught anes.
daft; lost the way	Poor hav'rel Will fell aff the drift,
cabbage	An' wandered thro' the bow-kail,
	An' pou't, for want o' better shift,
stalk	A runt was like a sow-tail,
so bent	Sae bow't that night.

VII

	The auld guidwife's weel-hoordet nits
	Are round an' round divided,
	An' monie lads' an' lasses' fates
	Are there that night decided:
snugly	Some kindle, couthie, side by side,
	An' burn thegither trimly;
	Some start awa, wi' saucy pride,
	An' jump out-owre the chimlie
	Fu' high that night.

VIII

attentive	Jean slips in twa, wi' tentie e'e;
	Wha 'twas, she wadna tell;
	But this is *Jock*, an' this is *me*,
	She says in to hersel:
	He bleez'd owre her, an' she owre him,
	As they wad never mair part,
chimney	Till fuff! he started up the lum,
	An' Jean had e'en a sair heart
	To see't that night.

XVII

Then up gat fechtin Jamie Fleck,
  An' he swoor by his conscience,
That he could saw hemp-seed a peck; sow
  For it was a' but nonsense:
The auld guidman raught down the reached;
    pock, bag
  An' out a handfu' gied him;
Syne bad him slip frae 'mang the folk, then
  Sometime when nae ane see'd him,
    An' try't that night.

XIX

He whistl'd up *Lord Lennox' March*,
  To keep his courage cheary;
Altho' his hair began to arch,
  He was sae fley'd an' eerie: frightened
Till presently he hears a squeak,
  An' then a grane an' gruntle; groan
He by his shouther gae a keek, glance
  An' tumbl'd wi' a wintle somersault
    Out-owre that night.

XX

He roar'd a horrid murder-shout,
  In dreadfu' desperation!
An' young an' auld came rinnin' out,
  To hear the sad narration:
He swore 'twas hilchin Jean M'Craw, limping
  Or crouchie Merran Humphie, hump-backed
Till stop! she trotted thro' them a';
  An' wha was it but *grumphie* the pig
    Asteer that night! astir

XXVIII

talks Wi' merry sangs, an' friendly cracks,
I wat they did na weary;
strange And unco tales, an' funnie jokes,
Their sports were cheap an' cheary:
a thin porridge; steam Till butter'd sow'ns, wi' fragrant lunt,
tongues wagging Set a' their gabs a-steerin';
liquor Syne, wi' a social glass o' strunt,
They parted aff careerin'
Fu' blythe that night.

ROBERT BURNS.

NOTES.—The first ceremony of Halloween is, pulling each a *Stock*, or plant of kail (greens). They must go out, hand in hand, with eyes shut, and pull the first they meet with: its being big or little, straight or crooked, is prophetic of the size and shape of the grand object of all their Spells—the husband or wife. Burning the nuts is a favourite charm. They name the lad and lass to each particular nut, as they lay them in the fire; and according as they burn quietly together, or start from beside one another, the course and issue of the Courtship will be. You should also go out secretly and sow a handful of hemp-seed. Look over your left shoulder, and you will see the appearance of him (or her) who is to be your true love in the attitude of pulling hemp.

THE BROWNIE OF BLEDNOCH

farmsteading THERE cam' a strange wight to our town-en',
devil; know And the fient a body did him ken;
rattled at the door He tirled na lang, but he glided ben
hesitation Wi' a dreary, dreary hum.

I trow the bauldest stood aback,
ears Wi' a gape and a glower till their lugs did crack,
As the shapeless phantom mum'ling spak',
"Ha'e ye wark for Aiken-drum?"

Roun' his hairy form there was naething seen
But a philabeg o' the rashes green, kilt ; rushes
And his knotted knees played aye knoit be- knocked together
tween ;
What a sight was Aiken-drum !

On his wauchie arms three claws did meet feeble, sallow
As they trailed on the grun' by his taeless
feet ;
E'en the auld gudeman himsel' did sweat
To look at Aiken-drum.

" I lived in a lan' where we saw nae sky,
I dwalt in a spot where a burn rins na not
by ;
But I'se dwall now wi' you if ye like to try—
Ha'e ye wark for Aiken-drum ?

" I'll shiel a' your sheep i' the mornin' sune, fold
I'll berry your crap by the light o' the thresh
moon,
And baa the bairns wi' an unken'd tune lull to sleep
If ye'll keep puir Aiken-drum.

" I'se seek nae guids, gear, bond nor mark ; property
I use nae beddin', shoon nor sark ;
But a cogfu' o' brose 'tween the light and dishful of porridge
dark
Is the wage o' Aiken-drum."

Quoth the wylie auld wife, " The thing speaks
weel ;
Our workers are scant—we ha'e routh o' meal ; plenty
Gif he'll do as he says—be he man, be he de'il, if
Wow ! we'll try this Aiken-drum."

Roun' a' that side what wark was dune
the Northern Lights — By the streamer's gleam or the glance o' the moon ;
A word or a wish—and the brownie cam' sune,
Sae helpfu' was Aiken-drum.

But he slade aye awa' ere the sun was up ;
Unorthodox persons betrayed themselves when handling this communion cup. — He ne'er could look straught on Macmillan's cup ;
They watched—but nane saw him his brose ever sup
Nor a spune sought Aiken-drum.

fastidious fancies — But a new-made wife, fu' o' rippish freaks,
tidy — Fond o' a' things feat for the first five weeks
Laid a mouldy pair o' her ain man's breeks
By the brose o' Aiken-drum.

Let the learned decide when they convene
What spell was him and the breeks between ;
For frae that day forth he was nae mair seen,
And sair missed was Aiken-drum.

shepherd ; a Farm — He was heard by a herd gaun by the *Thrieve*
weep — Crying, " Lang, lang now may I greet and grieve ;
For alas ! I ha'e gotten baith fee and leave,
O luckless Aiken-drum ! "

William Nicholson.

6. *War*

SCOTS, WHA HAE WI' WALLACE BLED

Scots, wha hae wi' Wallace bled,
Scots, wham Bruce has aften led;
Welcome to your gory bed,
Or to victorie!

Now's the day, and now's the hour;
See the front o' battle lour;
See approach proud Edward's power—
Chains and slaverie!

Wha will be a traitor-knave?
Wha will fill a coward's grave?
Wha sae base as be a slave?
Let him turn and flee!

Wha for Scotland's king and law
Freedom's sword will strongly draw,
Freeman stand, or freeman fa',
Let him follow me!

By oppression's woes and pains,
By your sons in servile chains,
We will drain our dearest veins,
But they shall be free.

Lay the proud usurpers low!
Tyrants fall in every foe!
Liberty's in ever blow!
Let us do, or dee!

Robert Burns.

THE TWA CORBIES

As I was walking all alane,
ravens; lament — I heard twa corbies making a mane:
The tane unto the t'other say,
"Whar sall we gang and dine the day?"

turf — "In ahint yon auld fail dyke
I wot there lies a new-slain knight;
And naebody kens that he lies there
But his hawk, his hound, and his lady fair.

"His hound is to the hunting gane,
His hawk to fetch the wild-fowl hame,
His lady has ta'en anither mate,
So we may mak' our dinner sweet.

neck — "Ye'll sit on his white hause-bane,
And I'll pike out his bonny blue e'en:
Wi' ae lock o' his gowden hair
thatch — We'll theek our nest when it grows bare.

"Mony a one for him maks mane,
But nane sall ken whar he is gane:
O'er his white banes, when they are bare,
The wind sall blaw for evermair."

MARCH, MARCH, ETTRICK AND TEVIOTDALE

MARCH, march, Ettrick and Teviotdale,
Why the deil dinna ye march forward in order?
March, march, Eskdale and Liddesdale,
All the Blue Bonnets are bound for the Border.

Many a banner spread,
Flutters above your head,
Many a crest that is famous in story.
Mount and make ready then,
Sons of the mountain glen,
Fight for the Queen and our old Scottish glory.

Come from the hills where your hirsels are grazing, flocks
Come from the glen of the buck and the roe;
Come to the crag where the beacon is blazing,
Come with the buckler, the lance, and the bow.
Trumpets are sounding,
War-steeds are bounding,
Stand to your arms then, and march in good order;
England shall many a day
Tell of the bloody fray,
When the Blue Bonnets came over the Border.

SIR WALTER SCOTT.

HARLAW

Now haud your tongue, baith wife and carle,
And listen, great and sma',
And I will sing of Glenallan's Earl
That fought on the red Harlaw.

The cronach's cried on Bennachie, lament for the dead
And doun the Don and a',
And hieland and lawland may mournfu' be
For the sair field of Harlaw.

They saddled a hundred milk-white steeds,
They hae bridled a hundred black,

armour With a chafron of steel on each horse's head,
And a good knight upon his back.

They hadna ridden a mile, a mile,
A mile but barely ten,
swaggering When Donald came branking down the brae
Wi' twenty thousand men.

Their tartans they were waving wide,
swords Their glaives were glancing clear,
The pibrochs rung frae side to side,
Would deafen ye to hear.

The great Earl in his stirrups stood,
That Highland host to see;
"Now here a knight that's stout and good
May prove a jeopardie:

"What would'st thou do, my squire so gay,
That rides beside my reyne,
Were ye Glenallan's Earl the day,
And I were Roland Cheyne?

"To turn the rein were sin and shame,
To fight were wond'rous peril;
What would ye do now, Roland Cheyne,
Were ye Glenallan's Earl?"

"Were I Glenallan's Earl this tide,
And ye were Roland Cheyne,
The spur should be in my horse's side,
And the bridle upon his mane.

"If they hae twenty thousand blades,
And we twice ten times ten,
Yet they hae but their tartan plaids,
And we are mail-clad men.

" My horse shall ride through ranks sae rude,
  As through the moorland fern,—
Then ne'er let the gentle Norman blude
  Grow cauld for Highland kerne."

SIR WALTER SCOTT.

THE FLOWERS OF THE FOREST

I'VE seen the smiling of fortune beguiling,
  I've felt all its favours, and found its decay :
Sweet was its blessing, kind its caressing,
  But now it is fled—it is fled far away.

I've seen the Forest adornéd the foremost
  With flowers of the fairest, most pleasant
    and gay,
Sae bonnie was their blooming, their scent the
    air perfuming,
  But now they are wither'd and a' wede away. **died**

I've seen the morning with gold the hills
    adorning,
  And the dread tempest roaring before part-
    ing day ;
I've seen the Tweed's silver streams, glitt'ring
    in the sunny beams,
  Grow drumlie and dark as they roll'd on **muddy**
    their way.

O fickle fortune ! why this cruel sporting ?
  Why thus perplex us, poor sons of a day ?
Thy frowns cannot fear me, thy smiles cannot
    cheer me,
  For the Flowers of the Forest are a' wede
    away.

ALISON RUTHERFORD.

THE BATTLE OF DUNBAR

THE small Town of Dunbar stands, high and windy, looking down over its herring-boats, over its grim old Castle now much honey-combed,—on one of those projecting rock-promontories with which that shore of the Frith of Forth is niched and vandyked, as far as the eye can reach. From the bottom of Belhaven bay to that of the next seabight St. Abb's-ward, the Town and its environs form a peninsula. Along the base of which peninsula, 'not much above a mile and a half from sea to sea,' Oliver Cromwell's Army, on Monday 2nd of September 1650, stands ranked, with its tents and Town behind it,—in very forlorn circumstances. This now is all the ground that Oliver is lord of in Scotland. His Ships lie in the offing, with biscuit and transport for him; but visible elsewhere in the Earth no help.

Landward as you look from the Town of Dunbar there rises, some short mile off, a dusky continent of barren heath Hills; the Lammermoor, where only mountain-sheep can be at home. The crossing of *which*, by any of its boggy passes, and brawling stream-courses, no Army, hardly a solitary Scotch Packman could attempt, in such weather. To the edge of these Lammermoor Heights, David Lesley has betaken himself; lies now along the outmost spur of them,—a long Hill of considerable height, which the Dunbar people call the Dun, Doon, or sometimes for fashion's sake the Down, adding to it the Teutonic *Hill* likewise, though *Dun* itself in old Celtic signifies Hill. On this Doon Hill lies David Lesley with the victorious Scotch Army, upwards of Twenty-thousand strong; with the

Committees of Kirk and Estates, the chief Dignitaries of the Country, and in fact the flower of what the pure Covenant in this the Twelfth year of its existence can still bring forth. There lies he since Sunday night, on the top and slope of this Doon Hill, with the impassable heath-continents behind him ; embraces, as within outspread tiger-claws, the base-line of Oliver's Dunbar peninsula ; waiting what Oliver will do. Cockburnspath with its ravines has been seized on Oliver's left, and made impassable ; behind Oliver is the sea ; in front of him Lesley, Doon Hill, and the heath-continent of Lammermoor. Lesley's force is of Three-and-twenty-thousand, in spirits as of men chasing, Oliver's about half as many, in spirits as of men chased. What is to become of Oliver ?

The base of Oliver's 'Dunbar Peninsula,' as we have called it (or Dunbar Pinfold where he is now hemmed in, upon 'an entanglement very difficult'), extends from Belhaven Bay on his right, to Brocksmouth House on his left ; 'about a mile and a half from sea to sea.' Brocksmouth House, the Earl (now Duke) of Roxburgh's mansion, which still stands there, his soldiers now occupy as their extreme post on the left. As its name indicates, it is the *mouth* or issue of a small Rivulet, or *Burn*, called *Brock*, *Brocksburn* ; which, springing from the Lammermoor, and skirting David Lesley's Doon Hill, finds its egress here into the sea. The reader who would form an image to himself of the great Tuesday 3rd of September 1650, at Dunbar, must note well this little *Burn*. It runs in a deep grassy glen, which the South-country Officers in those old Pamphlets describe as a 'deep *ditch*, forty feet in depth, and about as many in width,'—ditch dug out by the little Brook itself, and carpeted with greensward, in the course of long thousands of years.

It runs pretty close by the foot of Doon Hill; forms, from this point to the sea, the boundary of Oliver's position: his force is arranged in battle-order along the left bank of this Brocksburn, and its grassy glen; he is busied all Monday, he and his Officers, in ranking them there. 'Before sunrise on Monday' Lesley sent down his horse from the Hill-top, to occupy the other side of this Brook; 'about four in the afternoon' his train came down, his whole Army gradually came down; and they now are ranking themselves on the opposite side of Brocksburn, on rather narrow ground; cornfields, but swiftly sloping upwards to the steep of Doon Hill. This goes on, in the wild showers and winds of Monday 2nd September 1650, on both sides of the Rivulet of Brock. Whoever will begin the attack, must get across this Brook and its glen first; a thing of much disadvantage.

Behind Oliver's ranks, between him and Dunbar, stand his tents; sprinkled up and down, by battalions, over the face of this 'Peninsula'; which is a low though very uneven tract of ground; now in our time all yellow with wheat and barley in the autumn season, but at that date only partially tilled,—describable by Yorkshire Hodgson as a place of plashes and rough bent-grass; terribly beaten by showery winds that day, so that your tent will hardly stand. There was then but one Farm-house on this tract, where now are not a few: thither were Oliver's Cannon sent this morning; they had at first been lodged 'in the Church,' an edifice standing then as now somewhat apart, 'at the south end of Dunbar.' We have notice of only one other 'small house,' belike some poor shepherd's homestead, in Oliver's tract of ground: it stands close by the Brock Rivulet itself, and in the bottom of the little glen; at a place where the banks of it flatten themselves out into a slope passable for carts : this of course, as the one 'pass' in that quarter, it is highly important to seize. Pride and Lambert lodged 'six horse and fifteen foot' in this poor hut early in the morning : Lesley's horse came across, and drove them out ; killing some and 'taking three prisoners';—and so got possession of this pass and hut ; but did not keep it.

And now farther, on the great scale, we are to remark very specially that there is just one other 'pass' across the Brocksburn ; and this is precisely where the London road now crosses it ; about a mile east from the former pass, and perhaps two gunshots west from Brocksmouth House. There the great road then as now crosses the Burn of Brock ; the steep grassy glen, or 'broad ditch forty feet deep,' flattening itself out here once more into a passable slope : passable, but still steep on the southern or Lesley side, still mounting up there, with considerable acclivity, into a high table-ground, out of which the Doon Hill, as outskirt of the Lammermoor, a short mile to your right, gradually gathers itself. There, at this 'pass,' on and about the present London road, as you discover after long dreary dim examining, took place the brunt or essential agony of the Battle of Dunbar long ago.

'The Lord General about four o'clock,' say the old Pamphlets, 'went into the Town to take some refreshment,' a hasty late dinner, or early supper, whichever we may call it ; 'and very soon returned back.' Coursing about the field, with enough of things to order ; walking at last with Lambert in the Park or Garden of Brocksmouth House, he discerns that Lesley is astir on the Hill-side ; altering his position somewhat. That Lesley in fact is coming wholly down to the basis of the Hill, where his horse had been since sunrise: coming wholly down to the edge of the Brook and glen, among the sloping harvest-fields there; and also is bringing up his left wing of horse, most part of it, towards his right; edging himself, 'shogging,' as Oliver calls it, his whole line more and more to the right! His meaning is, to get hold of Brocksmouth House and the pass of the Brook there; after which it will be free to him to attack us when he will!—Lesley in fact considers, or at least the Committee of Estates and Kirk consider, that Oliver is lost; that, on the whole, he must not be left to retreat, but must be attacked and annihilated here. . . . In a word, Lesley descends, has been descending all day, and 'shogs' himself to the right,—urged, I believe, by manifold counsel, and by the nature of the case; and, what is equally important for us, Oliver sees him, and sees through him, in this movement of his.

At sight of this movement, Oliver suggests to Lambert standing by him, Does it not give *us* an advantage, if we, instead of him, like to begin the attack? Here is the Enemy's right wing coming out to the open space, free to be attacked on any side; and the main-battle hampered in narrow sloping ground between Doon Hill and the Brook, has no room to manœuvre or assist: beat this right wing where it now stands; take it in flank and front with an overpowering force,—it is driven upon its own main-battle, the whole Army is beaten? Lambert eagerly assents, 'had meant to say the same thing.' Monk, who comes up at the moment, likewise assents; as the other Officers do, when the case is set before them. It is the plan resolved upon for battle. The attack shall begin to-morrow before dawn.

And so the soldiers stand to their arms, or lie within instant reach of their arms, all night; being upon an engagement very difficult indeed. The night is wild and wet;—2nd of September means 12th by our calendar: the Harvest Moon wades deep among clouds of sleet and hail. Whoever has a heart for prayer, let him pray now, for the wrestle of death is at hand. Pray,—and withal keep his powder dry! And be ready for extremities, and quit himself like a man!—Thus they pass the night; making that Dunbar Peninsula and Brock Rivulet long memorable to me. We English have some tents; the Scots have none. The hoarse sea moans bodeful, swinging low and heavy against these whinstone bays; the sea and the tempests are abroad, all else asleep but we,—and there is One that rides on the wings of the wind.

Towards three in the morning the Scotch foot, by order of a Major-General say some, extinguish their matches, all but two in a company; cower under the corn-shocks, seeking some imperfect shelter and sleep. Be wakeful, ye English; watch, and pray, and keep your powder dry. About four o'clock comes order to my puddingheaded Yorkshire friend, that his regiment must mount and march straightway; his and various other regiments march, pouring swiftly to the left to Brocksmouth House, to the Pass over the Brock. With overpowering force let us storm the Scots right wing there; beat that, and all is beaten. Major Hodgson riding along, heard, he says, 'a Cornet praying in the night;' a company of poor men, I think, making worship there, under the void Heaven, before battle joined: Major Hodgson, giving his charge to a brother Officer, turned aside to listen for a minute, and worship and pray along with them; haply his last prayer on this Earth, as it might prove to be. But no: this Cornet prayed with such effusion as was wonderful; and imparted strength to my Yorkshire friend, who strengthened his men by telling them of it. And the Heavens, in their mercy, I think, have opened us a way of deliverance! The Moon gleams out, hard and blue, riding among hail-clouds; and over St. Abb's Head, a streak of dawn is rising.

And now is the hour when the attack should be, and no Lambert is yet here, he is ordering the line far to the right yet; and Oliver occasionally, in Hodgson's hearing, is impatient for him. The Scots too, on this wing, are awake; thinking to surprise us; there is their trumpet sounding, we heard it once; and Lambert, who was to lead the attack, is not here. The Lord General is impatient;—behold Lambert at last! The trumpets peal, shattering with fierce clangour Night's silence; the cannons awaken along all the Line: 'The Lord of Hosts! The Lord of Hosts!' On, my brave ones, on!—

The dispute 'on this right wing was hot and stiff, for three quarters of an hour.' Plenty of fire, from fieldpieces, snaphances, matchlocks, entertains the Scotch main-battle across the Brock;—poor stiffened men, roused from the corn-shocks with their matches all out! But here on the right, their horse, 'with lancers in the front rank,' charge desperately; drive us back across the hollow of the Rivulet;—back a little; but the Lord gives us courage, and we storm home again, horse and foot, upon them, with a shock like tornado tempests; break them, beat them, drive them all adrift. 'Some fled towards Copperspath, but most across their own foot.' Their own poor foot, whose matches were hardly well alight yet! Poor men, it was a terrible awakening for them: fieldpieces and charge of foot across the Brockburn; and now here is their own horse in mad panic trampling them to death. Above Three-thousand killed upon the place:

'I never saw such a charge of foot and horse,' says one, nor did I. Oliver was still near to Yorkshire Hodgson when the shock succeeded; Hodgson heard him say, "They run! I profess they run!" And over St. Abb's Head and the German Ocean, just then, bursts the first gleam of the level Sun upon us, 'and I heard Nol say, in the words of the Psalmist, "Let God arise, let His enemies be scattered,"'—or in Rous's metre,

> Let God arise, and scattered
> Let all his enemies be;
> And let all those that do him hate
> Before his presence flee!

Even so. The Scotch Army is shivered to utter ruin; rushes in tumultuous wreck, hither, thither; to Belhaven, or, in their distraction, even to Dunbar; the chase goes as far as Haddington; led by Hacker. 'The Lord General made a halt,' says Hodgson, 'and sang the Hundred-and-seventeenth Psalm,' till our horse could gather for the chase. Hundred-and-seventeenth Psalm, at the foot of the Doon Hill; there we uplift it, to the tune of Bangor, or some still higher score, and roll it strong and great against the sky:

> O give ye praise unto the Lord,
> All nati-ons that be;
> Likewise ye people all, accord
> His name to magnify!
> For great to-us-ward ever are
> His lovingkindnesses;
> His truth endures forevermore:
> The Lord O do ye bless!

And now to the chase again.

THOMAS CARLYLE.
(From *Letters and Speeches of Oliver Cromwell.*)

THE BURIAL-MARCH OF DUNDEE

Sound the fife, and cry the slogan—
  Let the pibroch shake the air
With its wild triumphal music,
  Worthy of the freight we bear.
Let the ancient hills of Scotland
  Hear once more the battle-song
Swell within their glens and valleys
  As the clansmen march along!
Never from the field of combat,
  Never from the deadly fray,
Was a nobler trophy carried
  Than we bring with us to-day . . .
Lo! we bring with us the hero—
  Lo! we bring the conquering Graeme,
Crowned as best beseems a victor
  From the altar of his fame . . .

On the heights of Killiecrankie
  Yester-morn our army lay:
Slowly rose the mist in columns
  From the river's broken way;
Hoarsely roared the swollen torrent,
  And the Pass was wrapt in gloom,
When the clansmen rose together
  From their lair amidst the broom.
Then we belted on our tartans,
  And our bonnets down we drew,
And we felt our broadswords' edges,
  And we proved them to be true;

And we prayed the prayer of soldiers,
  And we cried the gathering cry,
And we clasped the hands of kins-
    men,
  And we swore to do or die!
Then our leader rode before us
  On his war-horse black as night—
Well the Cameronian rebels
  Knew that charger in the fight!—
And a cry of exultation
  From the bearded warriors rose;
For we loved the house of Claver'se,
  And we thought of good Montrose.
But he raised his hand for silence—
  "Soldiers! I have sworn a vow:
Ere the evening star shall glisten
  On Schehallion's lofty brow,
Either we shall rest in triumph,
  Or another of the Graemes
Shall have died in battle-harness
  For his country and King James!
Think upon the Royal Martyr—
  Think of what his race endure—
Think of him whom butchers murdered
  On the field of Magus Muir:—
By his sacred blood I charge ye,
  By the ruined hearth and shrine—
By the blighted hopes of Scotland,
  By your injuries and mine—
Strike this day as if the anvil
  Lay beneath your blows the while,
Be they covenanting traitors,
  Or the brood of false Argyle!
Strike! and drive the trembling rebels
  Backwards o'er the stormy Forth;

Let them tell their pale Convention
  How they fared within the North.
Let them tell that Highland honour
  Is not to be bought nor sold,
That we scorn their prince's anger
  As we loathe his foreign gold.
Strike! and when the fight is over,
  If ye look in vain for me,
Where the dead are lying thickest,
  Search for him that was Dundee!"

Soon we heard a challenge trumpet
  Sounding in the Pass below,
And the distant tramp of horses,
  And the voices of the foe:
Down we crouched amid the bracken,
  Till the Lowland ranks drew near,
Panting like the hounds in summer,
  When they scent the stately deer.
From the dark defile emerging,
  Next we saw the squadrons come,
Leslie's foot and Leven's troopers
  Marching to the tuck of drum;
Through the scattered wood of birches,
  O'er the broken ground and heath,
Wound the long battalion slowly,
  Till they gained the plain beneath;
Then we bounded from our covert.—
  Judge how looked the Saxons then,
When they saw the rugged mountain
  Start to life with armèd men!
Like a tempest down the ridges
  Swept the hurricane of steel,
Rose the slogan of Macdonald—
  Flashed the broadsword of Locheill!

Vainly sped the withering volley
  'Mongst the foremost of our band—
On we poured until we met them,
  Foot to foot, and hand to hand.
Horse and man went down like drift-
    wood
  When the floods are black at Yule,
And their carcasses are whirling
  In the Garry's deepest pool.
Horse and man went down before us—
  Living foe there tarried none
On the field of Killiecrankie,
  When that stubborn fight was done!

And the evening star was shining
  On Schehallion's distant head,
When we wiped our bloody broad-
    swords,
  And returned to count the dead.
There we found him gashed and gory,
  Stretched upon the cumbered plain,
As he told us where to seek him,
  In the thickest of the slain.
And a smile was on his visage,
  For within his dying ear
Pealed the joyful note of triumph,
  And the clansmen's clamorous cheer:
So, amidst the battle's thunder,
  Shot, and steel, and scorching flame,
In the glory of his manhood
  Passed the spirit of the Graeme!

WILLIAM EDMONDSTOUNE AYTOUN.
(From *Lays of the Scottish Cavaliers.*)

7. *The Highlands*

THE ENCOUNTER AT ABERFOYLE

About half a mile's riding, after we crossed the bridge, placed us at the door of the public-house where we were to pass the evening. It was a hovel rather worse than better than that in which we had dined ; but its little windows were lighted up, voices were heard from within, and all intimated a prospect of food and shelter, to which we were by no means indifferent. Andrew was the first to observe that there was a peeled willow-wand placed across the half-open door of the little inn. He hung back, and advised us not to enter. ' For,' said Andrew, ' some of their chiefs and grit men are birling [1] at the usquebaugh in by there, and dinna want to be disturbed ; and the least we'll get, if we gang ram-stam in on them, will be a broken head, to learn us better havings, if we dinna come by the length of a cauld dirk in our wame,[2] whilk is just as likely."

I looked at the Bailie, who acknowledged, in a whisper, ' that the gowk [3] had some reason for singing, ance in the year.'

Meantime a staring half-clad wench or two came out of the inn and the neighbouring cottages, on hearing the sound of our horses' feet. No one bade us welcome, nor did any one offer to take our horses, from which we had alighted ; and to our various enquiries, the hopeless response of 'Ha niel Sassenach,' was the only answer we could extract. The Bailie, however, found (in his experience) a way to make them

[1] Drinking. [2] Belly. [3] Cuckoo.

speak English. 'If I gie ye a bawbee,' said he to an urchin of about ten years old, with a fragment of tattered plaid about him, 'will you understand Sassenach?'

"Ay, ay, that will I," replied the brat, in very decent English.

'Then gang and tell your mammy, my man, there's twa Sassenach gentlemen come to speak wi' her.'

The landlady presently appeared, with a lighted piece of split fir blazing in her hand. The turpentine in this species of torch (which is generally dug from out the turf-bogs) makes it blaze and sparkle readily, so that it is often used in the Highlands in lieu of candles. On this occasion such a torch illuminated the wild and anxious features of a female, pale, thin, and rather above the usual size, whose soiled and ragged dress, though aided by a plaid or tartan screen, barely served the purposes of decency, and certainly not those of comfort. Her black hair, which escaped in uncombed elf-locks from under her coif, as well as the strange and embarrassed look with which she regarded us, gave me the idea of a witch disturbed in her unlawful rites. She plainly refused to admit us into the house. We remonstrated anxiously, and pleaded the length of our journey, the state of our horses, and the certainty that there was not another place where we could be received nearer than Callander, which the Bailie stated to be seven Scots miles distant. How many these may exactly amount to in English measurement, I have never been able to ascertain, but I think the double *ratio* may be pretty safely taken as a medium computation. The obdurate hostess treated our expostulations with contempt. 'Better gang farther than fare waur,' she said, speaking the Scottish Lowland dialect, and being indeed a native of the

Lennox district—'Her house was ta'en up wi' them wadna like to be intruded on wi' strangers. She didna ken what mair might be there—redcoats, it might be, frae the garrison.' (These last words she spoke under her breath, and with very strong emphasis.) 'The night,' she said, 'was fair abune head—a night amang the heather wad caller [1] our bloods—we might sleep in our claes as mony a gude blade does in the scabbard—there wasna muckle flow-moss in the shaw,[2] if we took up our quarters right, and we might pit up our horses to the hill, naebody wad say naething against it.'

'But, my good woman,' said I, while the Bailie groaned and remained undecided, 'it is six hours since we dined, and we have not taken a morsel since. I am positively dying with hunger, and I have no taste for taking up my abode supperless among these mountains of yours. I positively must enter; and make the best apology you can to your guests for adding a stranger or two to their number. Andrew, you will see the horses put up.'

The Hecate looked at me with surprise, and then ejaculated, 'A wilfu' man will hae his way—them that will to Cupar maun to Cupar! To see thae English belly-gods—he has had ae fu' meal the day already, and he'll venture life and liberty rather than he'll want a het supper! Set roasted beef and pudding on the opposite side o' the pit o' Tophet and an Englishman will mak a spang [3] at it—But I wash my hands o't—Follow me, sir,' (to Andrew), 'and I'se show ye where to pit the beasts.'

I own I was somewhat dismayed at my landlady's expressions, which seemed to be ominous of some approaching danger. I did not, however, choose to

[1] Freshen. [2] Morass in the wood. [3] Leap.

shrink back after having declared my resolution, and accordingly I boldly entered the house; and after narrowly escaping breaking my shins over a turf back and a salting-tub, which stood on either side of the narrow exterior passage, I opened a crazy half-decayed door, constructed not of plank, but of wicker, and, followed by the Bailie, entered into the principal apartment of this Scottish caravansary.

The interior presented a view which seemed singular enough to southern eyes. The fire, fed with blazing turf and branches of dried wood, blazed merrily in the centre; but the smoke, having no means to escape but through a hole in the roof, eddied round the rafters of the cottage, and hung in sable folds at the height of about five feet from the floor. The space beneath was kept pretty clear, by innumerable currents of air which rushed towards the fire from the broken panel of basket-work which served as a door, from two square holes, designed as ostensible windows, through one of which was thrust a plaid, and through the other a tattered great-coat; and moreover, through various less distinguishable apertures, in the walls of the tenement, which, being built of round stones and turf, cemented by mud, let in the atmosphere at innumerable crevices.

At an old oaken table, adjoining the fire, sat three men, guests apparently, whom it was impossible to regard with indifference. Two were in the Highland dress; the one, a little dark-complexioned man, with a lively, quick, and irritable expression of features, wore the trews, or close pantaloons, wove out of a sort of chequered stocking stuff. The Bailie whispered me, that "he behoved to be a man of some consequence, for that naebody but their Duinhé-wassels [1] wore the

[1] Gentlemen.

trews ; they were ill to weave exactly to their Highland pleasure."

The other mountaineer was a very tall, strong man, with a quantity of reddish hair, freckled face, high cheek-bones, and long chin—a sort of caricature of the national features of Scotland. The tartan which he wore differed from that of his companions, as it had much more scarlet in it, whereas the shades of black and dark-green predominated in the chequers of the other. The third, who sate at the same table, was in the Lowland dress,—a bold, stout-looking man, with a cast of military daring in his eye and manner, his riding-dress showily and profusely laced, and his cocked hat of formidable dimensions. His hanger and a pair of pistols lay on the table before him. Each of the Highlanders had their naked dirks stuck upright in the board beside him,—an emblem, I was afterwards informed, but surely a strange one, that their compotation was not to be interrupted by any brawl. A mighty pewter measure, containing about an English quart of usquebaugh, a liquor nearly as strong as brandy, which the Highlanders distil from malt, and drink undiluted in excessive quantities, was placed before these worthies. A broken glass, with a wooden foot, served as a drinking cup to the whole party, and circulated with a rapidity, which, considering the potency of the liquor, seemed absolutely marvellous. These men spoke loud and eagerly together, sometimes in Gaelic, at other times in English. Another Highlander, wrapt in his plaid, reclined on the floor, his head resting on a stone from which it was only separated by a wisp of straw, and slept, or seemed to sleep, without attending to what was going on around him. He also was probably a stranger, for he lay in full dress, and accoutred with the sword and target, the usual arms of his countrymen when on a journey. Cribs there were of different dimensions beside the walls, formed, some of fractured boards, some of shattered wicker-work or plaited boughs, in which slumbered the family of the house, men, women, and children, their places of repose only concealed by the dusky wreaths of vapour which rose above, below, and around them.

Our entrance was made so quietly, and the carousers I have described were so eagerly engaged in their discussions, that we escaped their notice for a minute or two. But I observed the Highlander who lay beside the fire raise himself on his elbow as we entered, and, drawing his plaid over the lower part of his face, fix his look on us for a few seconds, after which he resumed his recumbent posture, and seemed again to betake himself to the repose which our entrance had interrupted.

We advanced to the fire, which was an agreeable spectacle after our late ride, during the chillness of an autumn evening among the mountains, and first attracted the attention of the guests who had preceded us, by calling for the landlady. She approached, looking doubtfully and timidly, now at us, now at the other party, and returned a hesitating and doubtful answer to our request to have something to eat.

" She didna ken," she said, " she wasna sure there was ony thing in the house," and then modified her refusal with the qualification,—" that is, ony thing fit for the like of us."

I assured her we were indifferent to the quality of our supper ; and looking round for the means of accommodation, which were not easily to be found, I arranged an old hen-coop as a seat for Mr. Jarvie, and turned down a broken tub to serve for my own. Andrew Fairservice entered presently afterwards, and took a place in silence behind our backs. The natives, as I may call them, continued staring at us, with an air as if confounded by our assurance, and we, at least I myself, disguised as well as we could, under an appearance of indifference, any secret anxiety we might feel concerning the mode in which we were to be received by those whose privacy we had disturbed.

At length, the lesser Highlander, addressing himself to me said, in very good English, and in a tone of great haughtiness, " Ye make yourself at home, sir, I see."

" I usually do so," I replied, " when I come into a house of public entertainment."

" And did she na see," replied the taller man, " by the white wand at the door, that gentlemans had taken up the public-house on their ain business ? "

" I do not pretend to understand the customs of this country ; but I am yet to learn," I replied, " how three persons should be entitled to exclude all other travellers from the only place of shelter and refreshment for miles round."

" There's nae reason for't, gentlemen," said the Bailie ; " we mean nae offence—but there's neither law nor reason for't—but as far as a stoup o' gude brandy wad make up the quarrel, we, being peaceable folk, wad be willing——"

" Damn your brandy, sir ! " said the Lowlander, adjusting his cocked-hat fiercely upon his head ; " we desire neither your brandy nor your company," and up he rose from his seat. His companions also rose, muttering to each other, drawing up their plaids, and snorting and snuffing the air after the manner of their countrymen when working themselves into a passion.

" I tauld ye what wad come, gentlemen," said the landlady, " an [1] ye wad hae been tauld—get awa' wi'

[1] If.

ye out o' my house, and make nae disturbance here—there's nae gentleman be disturbed at Jeanie MacAlpine's an she can hinder. A wheen [1] idle English loons, gaun about the country under cloud o' night, and disturbing honest peacable gentlemen that are drinking their drap drink at the fireside ! "

At another time I should have thought of the old Latin adage

> " Dat veniam corvis, vexat censura columbas——"

But I had not any time for classical quotation, for there was obviously a fray about to ensue, at which, feeling myself indignant at the inhospitable insolence with which I was treated, I was totally indifferent, unless on the Bailie's account, whose person and qualities were ill qualified for such an adventure. I started up, however, on seeing the others rise, and dropped my cloak from my shoulders, that I might be ready to stand on the defensive.

" We are three to three," said the lesser Highlander, glancing his eye at our party ; " if ye be pretty men, draw ! " and, unsheathing his broadsword, he advanced on me. I put myself in a posture of defence, and, aware of the superiority of my weapon, a rapier or small-sword, was little afraid of the issue of the contest. The Bailie behaved with unexpected mettle. As he saw the gigantic Highlander confront him with his weapon drawn, he tugged for a second or two at the hilt of his *shabble*, as he called it ; but finding it loth to quit the sheath, to which it had long been secured by rust and disuse, he seized, as a substitute, on the red-hot coulter of a plough which had been employed in arranging the fire by way of a poker, and brandished it with such effect, that at the first pass, he set the

[1] Few

Highlander's plaid on fire, and compelled him to keep a respectful distance till he could get it extinguished. Andrew, on the contrary, who ought to have faced the Lowland champion, had, I grieve to say it, vanished at the very commencement of the fray. But his antagonist, crying, " Fair play ! fair play ! " seemed courteously disposed to take no share in the scuffle. Thus we commenced our rencontre on fair terms as to numbers. My own aim was, to possess myself, if possible, of my antagonist's weapon ; but I was deterred from closing for fear of the dirk which he held in his left hand, and used in parrying the thrust of my rapier. Meantime the Bailie, notwithstanding the success of his first onset, was sorely bested. The weight of his weapon, the corpulence of his person, the very effervescence of his own passions were rapidly exhausting both his strength and his breath, and he was almost at the mercy of his antagonist, when up started the sleeping Highlander, from the floor on which he reclined, with his naked sword and target in his hand, and threw himself between the discomfited magistrate and his assailant, exclaiming, " Her nainsell has eaten the town pread at the Cross o' Glasgow, and py her troth she'll fight for Bailie Sharvie at the Clachan of Aberfoil—tat will she e'en ! " And seconding his words with deeds, this unexpected auxiliary made his sword whistle about the ears of his tall countryman, who, nothing abashed, returned his blows with interest. But being both accoutred with round targets made of wood, studded with brass, and covered with leather, with which they readily parried each other's strokes, their combat was attended with much more noise and clatter than serious risk of damage. It appeared, indeed that there was more of bravado than of serious attempt to do us any injury ; for the Lowland gentleman, who, as I mentioned, had stood aside for want of an antagonist when the brawl commenced, was now pleased to act the part of moderator and peace-maker.

"Haud your hands—haud your hands—eneugh done—eneugh done!—the quarrel's no mortal. The strange gentlemen have shown themselves men of honour, and gien reasonable satisfaction. I'll stand on mine honour as kittle[1] as ony man, but I hate unnecessary bloodshed."

It was not, of course, my wish to protract the fray—my adversary seemed equally disposed to sheath his sword—the Bailie, grasping for breath, might be considered as *hors de combat*, and our two sword-and-buckler men gave up their contest with as much indifference as they had entered into it.

"And now," said the worthy gentleman who acted as umpire, "let us drink and gree like honest fellows—The house will haud us a'. I propose that this good little gentleman that seems sair forfoughen,[2] as I may say, in this tuilzie, shall send for a tass o' brandy, and I'll pay for another, by way of archilowe,[3] and then we'll birl our bawbees[4] a' round about, like brethen."

"And fa's to pay my new ponnie plaid," said the larger Highlander, "wi' a hole burnt in't ane might put a kail-pat[5] through? Saw ever ony body a decent gentleman fight wi' a firebrand before?"

"Let that be nae hinderance," said the Bailie, who had now recovered his breath, and was at once disposed to enjoy the triumph of having behaved with spirit, and avoid the necessity of again resorting to such hard and doubtful arbitrement;—"Gin[6] I hae broken the

[1] Punctilious. [2] Worn out.
[3] Archilowe, of unknown derivation, signifies a peace-offering.
[4] Club our money for drink. [5] Broth-pot. [6] If.

head," he said, " I sall find the plaister. A new plaid sall ye hae, and o' the best—your ain clan-colours, man—an ye will tell me where it can be sent t'ye frae Glasco."

" I needna name my clan—I am of a king's clan, as is weel kend," said the Highlander ; " but ye may tak a bit o' the plaid—figh, she smells like a singit sheep's head !—and that'll learn ye the sett [1]—and a gentleman, that's a cousin o' my ain, that carries eggs doun frae Glencroe, will ca' for't about Martimas, an ye will tell her where ye bide. But, honest gentleman, neist time ye fight, an ye hae ony respect for your athversary, let it be wi' your sword, man, since ye ware ane, and no wi' thae het culters and fireprands, like a wild Indian."

" Conscience ! " replied the Bailie, " every man maun do as he dow [2]—my sword hasna seen the light since Bothwell Brigg, when my father, that's dead and gane, ware it ; and I kenna weel if it was forthcoming than either, for the battle was o' the briefest.—At ony rate, it's glewed to the scabbard now beyond my power to part them ; and, finding that, I e'en grippit at the first thing I could make a fend wi'. I trow my fighting days is done, though I like ill to take the scorn, for a' that.—But where's the honest lad that tuik my quarrel on himsell sae frankly ?—I'se bestow a gill o' aquavitæ on him, an I suld never ca' for anither."

The champion for whom he looked around was, however, no longer to be seen. He had escaped, unobserved by the Bailie, immediately when the brawl was ended, yet not before I had recognised, in his wild features and shaggy red hair, our acquaintance Dougal, the fugitive turnkey of the Glasgow jail. I communicated this observation in a whisper to the Bailie, who

[1] Pattern. [2] Can.

answered in the same tone, "Weel, weel, I see that him that ye ken o' said very right. There *is* some glimmering o' common sense about that creature Dougal; I maun see and think o' something will do him some gude."

Thus saying, he sat down, and fetching one or two deep aspirations, by way of recovering his breath, called to the landlady; "I think, Luckie, now that I find that there's nae hole in my wame, whilk I had muckle reason to doubt frae the doings o' your house, I wad be the better o' something to pit intill't."

Sir Walter Scott.
(From *Rob Roy*.)

THE HIGHLANDS BEFORE THE FORTY-FIVE

The Highlands are the Mountainous Parts of Scotland, not defined or described by any precise Limits or Boundaries of Counties or Shires but are Tracts of Mountains, in extent of Land, more than one-half of the Kingdom of Scotland; and are for the most part on the Western Ocean, extending from Dumbarton to the North End of the Island of Great Britain, near 200 Miles in length, and from about 40 to 80 Miles in breadth. All the Islands on the West and North-West Seas are called Highlands as well from their Mountainous Situation, as from the Habits, Customs, Manners and Language of their Inhabitants. The Lowlands are all that part of Scotland on the South of Forth and Clyde, and on the East side of the Kingdom from the Firth of Edinburgh to Caithness near the Orkneys is a Tract of Low Country from 4 to 20 Miles in Breadth.

The Number of Men able to carry Arms in the Highlands (including the Inhabitants of the Isles) is by the nearest Computation about 22,000 Men, of which Number about 10,000 are Vassals to the Superiors well affected to Your Majesty's Government; most of the remaining 12,000 have been engaged in Rebellion against Your Majesty, and are ready, whenever encouraged by their Superiors or Chiefs of Clans, to create new Troubles and rise in Arms in favour of the Pretender.

Their Notions of Virtue and Vice are very different from the more civilised part of Mankind. They think it is a most Sublime Virtue to pay a Servile and Abject Obedience to the Commands of their Chieftains, altho' in opposition to their Sovereign and the Laws of the Kingdom, and to encourage this, their Fidelity, they are treated by their Chiefs with great Familiarity, they partake with them in their Diversions, and shake them by the Hand wherever they meet them.

The Virtue next to this, in esteem amongst them, is the love they bear to that particular Branch of which they are a part, and in a Second Degree to the whole Clan, or Name, by assisting each other (right or wrong) against any other Clan with whom they are at Variance, and great Barbarities are often committed by One, to revenge the Quarrels of Another. They have still a more extensive adherence one to another as Highlanders in opposition to the People who inhabit the Low Countries, whom they hold in the utmost Contempt, imagining them inferior to themselves in Courage, Resolution, and the use of Arms, and accuse them of being Proud, Avaricious, and Breakers of their Word. They have also a Tradition amongst them that the Lowlands were in Ancient Times, the Inheritance of their Ancestors, and therefore believe they have a right to commit Depredations, whenever it is in their power to put them in Execution.

The Highlanders are divided into Tribes or Clans, under Lairds, or Chieftains (as they are called in the Laws of Scotland), each Tribe or Clan is subdivided into Little Branches sprung from the Main Stock who have also Chieftains over them, and from these are still smaller Branches of Fifty or Sixty Men, who deduce their Original from them, and on whom they rely as their Protectors and Defenders. The Arms they make use of in War, are, a Musket, a Broad Sword and Target, a Pistol and a Durk or Dagger, hanging by their side, with a Powder Horn and Pouch for their Ammunition. They form themselves into Bodies of unequal Numbers according to the strength of their Clan or Tribe, which is Commanded by their Respective Superior or Chieftain. When in sight of the Enemy they endeavour to possess themselves of the highest Ground, believing they descend on them with greater force.

They generally give their fire at a distance, they lay down their Arms on the Ground and make a Vigorous Attack with their Broad Swords, but if repulsed, seldom or never rally again. They dread engaging with the Cavalry and seldom venture to descend from the Mountains when apprehensive of being charged by them.

On sudden Alarms, or when any Chieftain is in distress, they give Notice to their Clans or those in Alliance with them, by sending a Man with what they call the Fiery Cross, which is a stick in the form of a Cross, burnt at the End, who send it forward to the next Tribe or Clan. They carry with it a written Paper directing them where to Assemble; upon sight of which they leave their Habitation and with great Expedition repair to the place of Rendezvous, with Arms, Ammunition and Meal for their Provision.

The Imposition..commonly called the Black Meal is levyed by the Highlanders on almost all the Low Country bordering thereon. But as it is equally Criminal by the Laws of Scotland to pay this Exaction or to Exort it the Inhabitants to avoid the Penalty of the Laws, agree with the Robbers, or some of their Correspondents in the Lowlands to protect their Horses and Cattle, who are in effect but their Stewards or Factors, and as long as this payment continues, the Depredations cease upon their Lands, otherwise the Collector of this Illegal Imposition is obliged to make good the loss they have sustained. They give regular Receipts for the same Safe Guard Money, and those who refuse to submit to this Imposition are sure of being Plundered, their being no other way to avoid it but by keeping a constant Guard of Armed Men, which, altho' it is sometimes done, is not only illegal, but a more expensive way of securing their property.

The Clans in the Highlands, the most addicted to Rapine and Plunder, are, the Cameron's on the West of the Shire of Inverness, the Mackenzie's and others in the Shire of Ross who were Vassals to the late Earl of Seaforth, the McDonell's of Keppoch, the Broadalbin Men, and the McGregors on the Borders of Argyleshire. They go out in Parties from Ten to Thirty Men, traverse large Tracts of Mountains till they arrive at the Lowlands where they Design to Commit Depredations, which they chuse to do in places distant from the Clans where they Inhabit; They drive the Stolen Cattle in the Night time, and in the Day remain on the Tops of the Mountains or in the Woods (with which the Highlands abound) and take the first occasion to sell them at the Fairs or Markets that are annually held in many parts of the Country.

(From *General Wade's Report on the Highlands*, 1724.)

BOSWELL AND DR. JOHNSON IN THE HIGHLANDS, 1773

A HIGHLAND HUT

We might have taken a chaise to Fort Augustus, but, had we not hired horses at Inverness, we should not have found them afterwards: so we resolved to begin here to ride. We had three horses, for Dr. Johnson, myself, and Joseph, and one which carried our portmanteaus, and two Highlanders who walked along with us, John Hay and Lauchland Vass, whom Dr. Johnson has remembered with credit in his *Journey*, though he has omitted their names. Dr. Johnson rode very well.

When we had advanced a good way by the side of Lochness, I perceived a little hut, with an old looking woman at the door of it. I thought here might be a scene that would amuse Dr. Johnson; so I mentioned it to him. "Let's go in," said he. We dismounted, and we and our guides entered the hut. It was a wretched little hovel of earth only, I think, and for a window had only a small hole, which was stopped with a piece of turf, that was taken out occasionally to let in light. In the middle of the room or space which we entered, was a fire of peat, the smoke going out at a hole in the roof. She had a pot upon it, with goat's flesh, boiling. There was at one end under the same roof, but divided by a kind of partition made of wattles, a pen or fold in which we saw a good many kids. I lighted a piece of paper, and went into the place where the bed was. There was a little partition of wicker, rather more neatly done than that for the fold, and close by the wall was a kind of bedstead of wood with heath upon it by way of bed ; at the foot of which I saw some sort of blankets or covering rolled up in a heap. The woman's name was Fraser ; so was her husband's. He was a man of eighty. Mr. Fraser of Balnain allows him to live in this hut, and keep sixty goats, for taking care of his woods, where he then was. They had five children, the eldest only thirteen. Two were gone to Inverness to buy meal ; the rest were looking after the goats. This contented family had four stacks of barley, twenty-four sheaves in each. They had a few fowls. We were informed that they lived all the spring without meal, upon milk and curds and whey alone. What they get for their goats, kids, and fowls, maintains them during the rest of the year.

She asked us to sit down and take a dram. I saw one chair. She said she was as happy as any woman in Scotland. She could hardly speak any English except a few detached words. Dr. Johnson was pleased at seeing, for the first time, such a state of human life. She asked for snuff. It is her luxury, and she uses a great deal. We had none ; but gave her sixpence a piece. She then brought out her whisky bottle. I tasted it ; as did Joseph and our guides : so I gave her sixpence more. She sent us away with many prayers in Erse.

HIGHLAND EMIGRATION

Between twelve and one we set out, and travelled eleven miles, through a wild country, till we came to a house in Glenmorison, called Anoch, kept by a M'Queen. The house here was built of thick turfs, and thatched with thinner turfs and heath. It had three rooms in length, and a little room which projected.

Where we sat, the side-walls were wainscotted, as Dr. Johnson said, with wicker, very neatly plaited. Our landlord had made the whole with his own hands.

After dinner, M'Queen sat by us a while, and talked with us. He said, all the Laird of Glenmorison's people would bleed for him, if they were well used ; but that seventy men had gone out of the Glen to America. That he himself intended to go next year ; for that the rent of his farm, which twenty years ago was only five pounds, was now raised to twenty pounds. That he could pay ten pounds, and live ; but no more.—Dr. Johnson said, he wished M'Queen laird of Glenmorison, and the laird to go to America. M'Queen very generously answered, he should be very sorry for it ; for the laird could not shift for himself in America as he could do.

BREAKFAST AT RAASAY

At breakfast this morning, among a profusion of other things, there were oat-cakes, made of what is called *gradaned* meal, that is, meal made of grain separated from the husks, and toasted by fire, instead of being threshed and kiln dried.—This seems to be bad management, as so much fodder is consumed by it. Mr. M'Queen however defended it, by saying, that it is doing the same thing much quicker, as one operation effects what is otherwise done by two. His chief reason however was, that the servants in Sky are, according to him, a faithless pack, and steal what they can ; so that much is saved by the corn passing but once through their hands, as at each time they pilfer some. It appears to me, that the gradaning is a strong proof of the laziness of the Highlanders, who will rather make fire act for them, at the expence of fodder, than labour themselves. There was also, what I cannot help disliking at breakfast, cheese: it is the custom over all the Highlands to have it; and it often smells very strong, and poisons to a certain degree the elegance of an Indian repast.

FLORA MACDONALD

I was highly pleased to see Dr. Johnson safely arrived at Kingsburgh, and received by the hospitable Mr. Macdonald, who, with a most respectful attention, supported him into the house. Kingsburgh was completely the figure of a gallant Highlander,—exhibiting "the graceful mien and manly looks," which our popular Scotch song has justly attributed to that character. He had his Tartan plaid thrown about him, a large blue bonnet with a knot of black ribband like a cockade, a brown short coat of a kind of duffil, a Tartan waistcoat with gold buttons and gold buttonholes, a bluish philibeg, and Tartan hose. He had jet black hair tied behind, and was a large stately man, with a steady sensible countenance.

There was a comfortable parlour with a good fire, and a dram went round. By and by supper was served, at which there appeared the lady of the house, the celebrated Miss Flora Macdonald. She is a little woman, of a genteel appearance, and uncommonly mild and well bred. To see Dr. Samuel Johnson, the great champion of the English Tories, salute Miss Flora Macdonald in the isle of Sky, was a striking sight; for though somewhat congenial in their notions, it was very improbable they should meet here. . . .

I slept in the same room with Dr. Johnson. Each had a neat bed, with Tartan curtains, in an upper chamber. The room where we lay was a celebrated one. Dr. Johnson's bed was the very bed in which the grandson of the unfortunate King James the Second lay, on one of the nights after the failure of his rash attempt in 1745-46, while he was eluding the pursuit of the emissaries of government, which had offered thirty thousand pounds as a reward for apprehending him. To see Dr. Samuel Johnson lying in that bed, in the isle of Sky, in the house of Miss Flora Macdonald, struck me with such a group of ideas as it is not easy for words to describe, as they passed through the mind. He smiled and said, " I have had no ambitious thoughts in it."

JAMES BOSWELL.
(From *The Journal of a Tour to the Hebrides.*)

8. Parting and Exile

AE FOND KISS

AE fond kiss, and then we sever ! one
Ae fareweel and then for ever !
Deep in heart-wrung tears I'll pledge thee,
Warring sighs and groans I'll wage thee.

Had we never loved sae kindly,
Had we never loved sae blindly,
Never met—or never parted,
We had ne'er been broken-hearted.

Fare thee weel, thou first and fairest !
Fare thee weel, thou best and dearest !
Thine be ilka joy and treasure, every
Peace, enjoyment, love and pleasure !

Ae fond kiss, and then we sever!
Ae fareweel, alas! for ever!
Deep in heart-wrung tears I'll pledge
thee,
Warring sighs and groans I'll wage thee.

ROBERT BURNS.

BLOWS THE WIND TO-DAY

BLOWS the wind to-day, and the sun and the
rain are flying,
Blows the wind on the moors to-day and
now,
Where about the graves of the martyrs the
whaups are crying,
My heart remembers how!

Grey recumbent tombs of the dead in desert
places,
Standing stones on the vacant wine-red
moor,
Hills of sheep, and the homes of the silent
vanished races,
And winds, austere and pure:

Be it granted me to behold you again in dying,
Hills of home! and to hear again the
call;
Hear about the graves of the martyrs the
peewees crying,
And hear no more at all.

ROBERT LOUIS STEVENSON.

IT WAS A' FOR OUR RIGHTFU' KING

It was a' for our rightfu' king all
We left fair Scotland's strand ;
It was a' for our rightfu' king,
We e'er saw Irish land, my dear,
We e'er saw Irish land.

Now a' is done that men can do,
And a' is done in vain :
My love and native land fareweel,
For I maun cross the main, my dear,
For I maun cross the main.

He turn'd him right, and round about,
Upon the Irish shore,
And gae his bridle-reins a shake, gave
With adieu for evermore, my dear,
With adieu for evermore !

The soger frae the wars returns,
The sailor frae the main,
But I hae parted frae my love,
Never to meet again, my dear,
Never to meet again.

When day is gane, and night is come,
And a' folk bound to sleep ;
I think on him that's far awa',
The lee-lang night, and weep, my dear, live-long
The lee-lang night, and weep.

ROBERT BURNS.

CANADIAN BOAT SONG

FAIR these broad meads—these hoary woods are grand ;
But we are exiles from our fathers' land.

Listen to me, as when you heard our father
Sing long ago the song of other shores—
Listen to me, and then in chorus gather
All your deep voices, as ye pull your oars.

From the lone sheiling of the misty island
Mountains divide us, and the waste of seas—
Yet still the blood is strong, the heart is Highland,
And we in dreams behold the Hebrides.

We ne'er shall tread the fancy-haunted valley,
Where 'tween the dark hills creeps the small clear stream,
In arms around the patriarch banner rally,
Nor see the moon on royal tombstones gleam.

When the bold kindred, in the time long vanish'd,
Conquered the soil and fortified the keep—
No seer foretold the children would be banish'd
That a degenerate lord might boast his sheep.

Come foreign rage—let Discord burst in slaughter !
O then for clansmen true, and stern claymore—
The hearts that would have given their blood like water,
Beat heavily beyond the Atlantic roar.

ANONYMOUS.

9. Burns and Scott

BURNS'S POEMS

At the time when the poet made his appearance and great first success, his work was remarkable in two ways. For, first, in an age when poetry had become abstract and conventional, instead of continuing to deal with shepherds, thunderstorms, and personifications, he dealt with the actual circumstances of his life, however matter-of-fact and sordid these might be. And, second, in a time when English versification was particularly stiff, lame, and feeble, and words were used with ultra-academical timidity, he wrote verses that were easy, racy, graphic, and forcible, and used language with absolute tact and courage as it seemed most fit to give a clear impression. If you take even those English authors whom we know Burns to have most admired and studied, you will see at once that he owed them nothing but a warning. Take Shenstone, for instance, and watch that elegant author as he tries to grapple with the facts of life. He has a description, I remember, of a gentleman engaged in sliding or walking on thin ice, which is a little miracle of incompetence. You see my memory fails me, and I positively cannot recollect whether his hero was sliding or walking; as though a writer should describe a skirmish, and the reader, at the end, be still uncertain whether it were a charge of cavalry or a slow and stubborn advance of foot. There could be no such ambiguity in Burns; his work is at the opposite pole from such indefinite and stammering performances;

and a whole lifetime passed in the study of Shenstone would only lead a man further and further from writing the *Address to a Louse.* Yet Burns, like most great artists, proceeded from a school and continued a tradition ; only the school and tradition were Scotch, and not English. While the English language was becoming daily more pedantic and inflexible, and English letters more colourless and slack, there was another dialect in the sister country, and a different school of poetry tracing its descent, through King James I., from Chaucer. The dialect alone accounts for much ; for it was then written colloquially, which kept it fresh and supple ; and, although not shaped for heroic flights, it was a direct and vivid medium for all that had to do with social life. Hence, whenever Scotch poets left their laborious imitations of bad English verses, and fell back on their own dialect, their style would kindle, and they would write of their convivial and somewhat gross existences with pith and point. In Ramsay, and far more in the poor lad Fergusson, there was mettle, humour, literary courage, and a power of saying what they wished to say definitely and brightly, which in the latter case should have justified great anticipations. Had Burns died at the same age as Fergusson, he would have left us literally nothing worth remark. To Ramsay and to Fergusson, then, he was indebted in a very uncommon degree, not only following their tradition and using their measures, but directly and avowedly imitating their pieces. The same tendency to borrow a hint, to work on some one else's foundation, is notable in Burns from first to last, in the period of song-writing as well as in that of the early poems ; and strikes one oddly in a man of such deep originality, who left so strong a print on all he touched, and whose work is so greatly distinguished by that character of "inevitability" which Wordsworth denied to Goethe.

When we remember Burns's obligations to his predecessors, we must never forget his immense advances on them. They had already "discovered" nature; but Burns discovered poetry—a higher and more intense way of thinking of the things that go to make up nature, a higher and more ideal key of words in which to speak of them. Ramsay and Fergusson excelled at making a popular—or shall we say vulgar?—sort of society verses, comical and prosaic, written, you would say, in taverns while a supper party waited for its laureate's word; but on the appearance of Burns, this coarse and laughing literature was touched to finer issues, and learned gravity of thought and natural pathos.

What he had gained from his predecessors was a direct, speaking style, and to walk on his own feet instead of on academical stilts. There was never a man of letters with more absolute command of his means; and we may say of him, without excess, that his style was his slave. Hence that energy of epithet, so concise and telling, that a foreigner is tempted to explain it by some special richness or aptitude in the dialect he wrote. Hence that Homeric justice and completeness of description which gives us the very physiognomy of nature, in body and detail, as nature is. Hence, too, the unbroken literary quality of his best pieces, which keeps him from any slip into the weariful trade of word-painting, and presents everything, as everything should be presented by the art of words, in a clear, continuous medium of thought. Principal Shairp, for instance, gives us a paraphrase of one tough verse of the original; and for those who know the Greek poets only by paraphrase, this has the very quality they are accustomed to look for and admire in Greek. The contemporaries of Burns were surprised that he should visit so many celebrated mountains and waterfalls, and not seize the opportunity to make a poem. Indeed, it is not for those who have a true command of the art of words, but for peddling, professional amateurs, that these pointed occasions are most useful and inspiring. As those who speak French imperfectly are glad to dwell on any topic they may have talked upon or heard others talk upon before, because they know appropriate words for it in French, so the dabbler in verse rejoices to behold a waterfall, because he has learned the sentiment and knows appropriate words for it in poetry. But the dialect of Burns was fitted to deal with any subject ; and whether it was a stormy night, a shepherd's collie, a sheep struggling in the snow, the conduct of cowardly soldiers in the field, the gait and cogitations of a drunken man, or only a village cockcrow in the morning, he could find language to give it freshness, body, and relief. He was always ready to borrow the hint of a design, as though he had a difficulty in commencing—a difficulty, let us say, in choosing a subject out of a world which seemed all equally living and significant to him ; but once he had the subject chosen, he could cope with nature single-handed, and make every stroke a triumph. Again, his absolute mastery in his art enabled him to express each and all of his different humours, and to pass smoothly and congruously from one to another. Many men invent a dialect for only one side of their nature—perhaps their pathos or their humour, or the delicacy of their senses—and, for lack of a medium, leave all the others unexpressed. You meet such a one, and find him in conversation full of thought, feeling, and experience, which he has lacked the art to employ in his writings. But Burns was not thus hampered in the practice of the literary art; he could throw the whole weight of his nature into his work, and impregnate it from end to end. If Doctor Johnson, that stilted and accomplished stylist, had lacked the sacred Boswell, what should we have known of him? and how should we have delighted in his acquaintance as we do? Those who spoke with Burns tell us how much we have lost who did not. But I think they exaggerate their privilege: I think we have the whole Burns in our possession set forth in his consummate verses.

It was by his style, and not by his matter, that he affected Wordsworth and the world. There is, indeed, only one merit worth considering in a man of letters—that he should write well; and only one damning fault—that he should write ill. We are little the better for the reflections of the sailor's parrot in the story. And so, if Burns helped to change the course of literary history, it was by his frank, direct, and masterly utterance, and not by his homely choice of subjects. That was imposed upon him, not chosen upon a principle. He wrote from his own experience, because it was his nature so to do, and the tradition of the school from which he proceeded was fortunately not opposed to homely subjects. But to these homely subjects he communicated the rich commentary of his nature; they were all steeped in Burns; and they interest us not in themselves, but because they have been passed through the spirit of so genuine and vigorous a man. Such is the stamp of living literature; and there was never any more alive than that of Burns.

What a gust of sympathy there is in him sometimes flowing out in byways hitherto unused, upon mice, and flowers, and the devil himself; sometimes speaking plainly between human hearts; sometimes ringing out in exultation like a peal of bells! When we compare the *Farmer's Salutation to his Auld Mare Maggie*, with the clever and inhumane production of half a century earlier, *The Auld Man's Mare's dead*, we see in a nut-shell the spirit of the change introduced by Burns. And as to its manner, who that has read it can forget how the collie, Luath, in the *Twa Dogs*, describes and enters into the merry-making in the cottage?

> "The luntin'[1] pipe an' sneeshin' mill,[2]
> Are handed round wi' richt guid will;
> The canty[3] auld folks crackin' crouse,[4]
> The young anes rantin'[5] through the house—
> My heart has been sae fain to see them
> That I for joy hae barkit wi' them."

It was this ardent power of sympathy that was fatal to so many women, and, through Jean Armour, to himself at last. His humour comes from him in a stream so deep and easy that I will venture to call him the best of humorous poets. He turns about in the midst to utter a noble sentiment or a trenchant remark on human life, and the style changes and rises to the occasion. I think it is Principal Shairp who says, happily, that Burns would have been no Scotchman if he had not loved to moralise; neither, may we add, would he have been his father's son; but (what is worthy of note) his moralisings are to a large extent the moral of his own career. He was among the least impersonal of artists. Except in the *Jolly Beggars*, he shows no gleam of dramatic instinct. Mr. Carlyle has complained that *Tam o' Shanter* is, from the absence of this quality, only a picturesque and external piece of

[1] Smoking. [2] Snuff-box. [3] Cheery. [4] Talking merrily. [5] Romping.

work ; and I may add that in the *Twa Dogs* it is precisely in the infringement of dramatic propriety that a great deal of the humour of the speeches depends for its existence and effect. Indeed, Burns was so full of his identity that it breaks forth on every page ; and there is scarce an appropriate remark either in praise or blame of his own conduct, but he has put it himself into verse. Alas ! for the tenor of these remarks ! They are, indeed, his own pitiful apology for such a marred existence and talents so misused and stunted ; and they seem to prove for ever how small a part is played by reason in the conduct of man's affairs. Here was one, at least, who with unfailing judgment predicted his own fate ; yet his knowledge could not avail him, and with open eyes he must fulfil his tragic destiny. Ten years before the end he had written his epitaph ; and neither subsequent events, nor the critical eyes of posterity, have shown us a word in it to alter. And, lastly, has he not put in for himself the last unanswerable plea ?—

> " Then gently scan your brother man,
>   Still gentler sister woman ;
> Though they may gang a kennin' wrang,
>   To step aside is human :
> One point must still be greatly dark——"

One ? Alas ! I fear every man and woman of us is " greatly dark " to all their neighbours, from the day of birth until death removes them, in their greatest virtues as well as in their saddest faults ; and we, who have been trying to read the character of Burns, may take home the lesson and be gentle in our thoughts.

ROBERT LOUIS STEVENSON.
(From *Men and Books.*)

SIR WALTER SCOTT

Mr. Balfour said well in the Chapter House of Westminster Abbey, that happy as was Sir Walter Scott's style in so painting his large canvases as to give us an adequate conception of the most striking scenes of a long past, it was not mainly in his style, but in the matter of his inimitable stories, that he has surpassed all the other writers of English romance. It is true enough that Scott represented, and represented as no other writer has ever represented, the reaction against the abstract doctrines of the eighteenth century, and substituted for them the concrete and rich detail of which his imagination was so full. But by that very capacity for combining all the glow and colour of a picturesque past with the concrete historic figures and vivacity of detail in which that past life attained its greatest dignity and interest, Scott deviated from the earlier conception of romance and mingled with it the criticism of a broad sagacity and the business insight of a shrewd realist. Sir Walter hardly ever takes us into a dull world, but nevertheless never into an unreal or abstract world. His history is, as Mr. Balfour said, often inaccurate ; indeed, it was usually made intentionally so, that he might give a more concentrated picture of that which struck his own imagination most powerfully. His inaccuracy was almost always of a kind which gave the impression of the truth far better than the most painstaking accuracy ever could have given it. Indeed, so far as I differ from Mr. Balfour at all, it would be in doubting whether Scott did depend so much on the opportuneness of his gifts for the special temper of the world in which he lived, as

Mr. Balfour suggests. It may well be that the genius of some men is so great that they really *create* the demand for what they can bestow. And of these Sir Walter Scott seems to me one of the most conspicuous. There is something so large and simple in his genius that his readers hardly think of themselves as readers of mere romance. The peasants are drawn as vividly as the kings, and the kings as the peasants. His readers are admitted to the very heart of reality, even when the romantic touch is most vigorous.

Scott never gives you the sense of confining his interest to his story. There is always a lifelike background, a sense of the largeness and complexity of human life, of its business, and of its manifold enterprises clashing against each other, which takes you out of the narrow interests of passion and mere adventure. In *Kenilworth* we have Queen Elizabeth playing off her nobles against each other as only a great Queen could do it ; in *The Fortunes of Nigel* the fussy and timid James consoles himself for his own conscious weakness by displaying gleams of shrewdness even when he is cowering before his own courtiers ; in *The Heart of Midlothian* a canny Scotch nobleman avails himself of Queen Caroline's deep sense of what was in the larger sense expedient because it was just, and just because it was expedient, to obtain a pardon for the sister of the heroine ; in *Ivanhoe* a most picturesque contrast is drawn between the crafty dealings of the great order of the Templars and the heavy Saxon nobles with their clumsy strength and dull straightforwardness ; in *Old Mortality* the mind is fixed on the contest between the stern Puritan fanatics and the military coldbloodedness of Claverhouse and his soldiers ; in *Anne of Geierstein,* the heart-broken pride of Margaret of Anjou dying in the midst of King

René's vain and shallow and tinselled court is painted with singular force. Everywhere in Scott's stories you see a large background depicting the real affairs of the world, and you feel as if you were moving amidst the bewildering paradoxes of human nature on a large scale, and not on the narrow stage of mere adventure or romance.

Nor is it in the field of the greater historic exploits alone that you feel the touch of a vivid realism. Not only is Louis XI. pictured in all his courage and craft and superstition, overfinessing his own hand in his eagerness to master the mad rages of his powerful vassal, Charles the Bold, but in the very same story we have the most lively picture of the singular combination of cold treachery and tenacious gratitude in the tribes of gipsies who were just then spreading over Europe; and, again, the rashness and shrewdness of those great Flemish burghers who, with all their keenness for commercial gain, were so arrogant and heady as to risk all their wealth on the fortunes of an unequal contest with the great military power of Burgundy, in credulous reliance on the secret promises of a wily French King who never hesitated to sacrifice an ally when he failed to mature his crafty schemes, is set before us with equal power. Again, what could be more striking than Scott's intimacy with all the details of the life of the poor, when he paints the toil and griefs of the poor fishermen and fisherwomen on the coast of Fife, or the dumb fidelity of the Saxon serf, or the struggles in the heart of the father of Jeanie and Effie Deans, when he has to choose between love for his daughter and fidelity to his religion; or the humours of the Scotch vagrant, Edie Ochiltree, or the didactic conceit and selfish unscrupulousness of the Pharisaic gardener, Andrew Fairservice? Scott is as much at home with the serving-men as he is with the Queens and Kings with whom his imagination delighted to busy itself. Everywhere you see large glimpses of the real world through the spacious windows of his glowing mind and memory. He is as familiar with the kitchen of the palace as he is with its Court. The Earl of Murray's menials are as powerfully suggested as his grim counsellors and jealous rivals, and James I.'s cook is almost as necessary a figure in the picture of his Court at Westminster as is Buckingham or Prince Charles. This it is which makes Scott's romances so much more fascinating than ordinary novels. They fill you with the sense of the greatness and complexity of the world, and yet they never weary you with those long digressions with which the more ambitious writers of romance try to fill in the background of their story. Compare Scott's stories, for instance, with Bulwer's *Last Days of Pompeii*, or *Last of the Barons*, and you see immediately the vast superiority of the former in mingling the realities of life with the glow of passion and the charm of pageant.

Of course it is quite true that Scott is not always at his best. Walking ladies and gentlemen, like Rowena in *Ivanhoe*, or Isabella Wardour in *The Antiquary*, glide through his pages and hardly leave a trace on the memory. The humour of his "Introductions," as well as of the tags to which his oddities are addicted, is often overweighted, is often heavy. I weary of his Jedediah Cleishbottom, and even of Lady Margaret Bellenden in her castle of Tillietudlem. Nor are his semi-supernatural personages like Meg Merrilies and Magdalen Graeme as impressive as they ought to be. But yet he has a great genius for that touch of madness which makes both his daft Scotch boys, and his pictures of genuine mental excitement, like that of Madge

Wildfire, so effective. There was a harebrained element in Scott that when it really took possession of him was full of eeriness, all the more that his great breadth of sober sense threw it out with singularly vivid force. There is nothing more powerful than his picture of Mary Stuart's mind in *The Abbot* when it gets unhinged in recalling the tragedies of her earlier life ; or than the scenes in the *Bride of Lammermoor*, where Lucy Ashton's anguish turns her brain. Even in his own life, in the journal which he kept of his private dreads and sufferings, one sees traces of the fire of that great imagination when it carried him beyond the control of his cool and lucid judgment. Without that strain of wildness in Scott which showed itself in such despair as the motto which he wrote when he first realised the failing of his genius, in *Count Robert of Paris*, we should never have had the greatest of all our imaginative writers excepting only Shakespeare : —

> The storm increases—'tis no sunny shower
> Fostered in the moist breast of March or April,
> Or such as parched Summer cools his lip with ;
> Heaven's windows are flung wide ; the inmost deeps
> Call, in hoarse greetings, one upon another ;
> On comes the flood in all its foaming horrors,
> And where's the dike shall stop it ?

There, and in the burst of chivalrous feeling that suggested the verse,—

> Sound, sound the Clarion, fill the fife,
> To all the sensual world proclaim
> One crowded hour of glorious life
> Is worth a world without a name,—

we have the touch of fire that electrified into living and moving forms all the massive contents of that great mind,—and that went far towards shattering his earthly happiness while it secured his everlasting fame.

RICHARD HOLT HUTTON. (From *Brief Literary Criticisms.*)

10. Love and Loyalty

I WILL MAKE YOU BROOCHES

I WILL make you brooches and toys for your
delight
Of bird-song at morning and star-shine at
night.
I will make a palace fit for you and me
Of green days in forests and blue days at
sea.

I will make my kitchen, and you shall keep
your room,
Where white flows the river and bright blows
the broom,
And you shall wash your linen and keep your
body white
In rainfall at morning and dewfall at night.

And this shall be for music when no one else
is near,
The fine song for singing, the rare song to
hear!
That only I remember, that only you
admire,
Of the broad road that stretches and the
roadside fire.

ROBERT LOUIS STEVENSON.

BUT WE'LL GROW AULD THEGITHER

together — BUT we'll grow auld thegither and ne'er find
The loss o' youth where love grows on the mind.
Bairns and their bairns make sure a firmer tie
anything — Than ocht in love the like o' us can spy.
See yon twa elms that grow up side by side :
since, ago — Suppose them some years syne bridegroom and bride ;
every — Nearer and nearer ilka year they've pressed
Till wide their spreadin' branches are increased
now — An' in their mixture noo are fully blest :
This shields the ither frae the eastlin' blast :
That in return defends it frae the wast.
such — Sic as stand single (a state liked by you)
direction — Beneath ilk storm frae every airt maun bow.

ALAN RAMSAY.
(From *The Gentle Shepherd.*)

THEIR GROVES O' SWEET MYRTLE

THEIR groves o' sweet myrtle let foreign lands reckon,
Where bright-beaming summers exalt the perfume ;
Far dearer tae me yon lone glen o' green breckan, — bracken
Wi' the burn stealin' under the lang yellow broom.
Far dearer tae me yon humble broom bowers,
daisy — Where the blue-bell and gowan lurk, lowly, unseen.

ROBERT BURNS.

AULD LANG SYNE

SHOULD auld acquaintance be forgot
  And never brought to mind?
Should auld acquaintance be forgot,
  And auld lang syne?   long ago

For auld lang syne, my dear,
  For auld lang syne,
We'll tak a cup o' kindness yet
  For auld lang syne.

And surely you'll be your pint-stowp,   pay for
  And surely I'll be mine;
And we'll tak a cup o' kindness yet
  For auld lang syne.

We twa hae run about the braes,
  And pu'd the gowans fine;   pulled; daisies
But we've wander'd mony a weary fit,   foot
  Sin' auld lang syne.   since

We twa hae paidl'd in the burn,   waded
  Frae morning sun till dine;   noon
But seas between us braid hae roar'd,   broad
  Sin' auld lang syne.

And there's a hand, my trusty fiere!   crony
  And gie's a hand o' thine!   give me
And we'll tak a right guid-willie waught   hearty draught of goodwill
  For auld lang syne!

ROBERT BURNS.

AULD ROBIN GRAY

fold *cows* WHEN the sheep are in the fauld, and the kye's a' at hame,
And a' the world to rest are gane,
woes The waes o' my heart fa' in showers frae my e'e,
unknown Unkent by my gudeman, wha sleeps sound by me.

Young Jamie lo'ed me weel, and ask'd me for his bride,
But saving a crown, he had naething else beside;
To make the crown a pound, my Jamie gaed to sea,
And the crown and the pound, they were baith for me.

He hadna been gane a week but only twa,
When my faither brake his arm, and our cow *stolen* was stown awa';
My mither she fell sick—and my Jamie at the sea—
And auld Robin Gray came a-courting me.

My faither couldna work, and my mither couldna spin;
I toil'd day and night, but their bread I couldna win;
Auld Rob maintain'd them baith, and wi' tears in his e'e,
Said, "Jenny, for their sakes will ye no' marry me?"

My heart it said nay, and I looked for Jamie
back;
But the wind it blew high, and the ship was
a wrack;
The ship it was a wrack—why didna Jamie
dee?
And why do I live to say, Wae's me!

My faither urged me sair, my mither didna
speak,
But she looked in my face till my heart was
like to break;
So I gied him my hand though my heart was
on the sea,
And auld Robin Gray was gudeman to me.

I hadna been a wife a week but only four,
When, mournfu' as I sat on the stane at the
door,
I saw my Jamie's wraith, for I couldna think
it he,
Till he said, "I'm come back, love, to marry
thee."

O! sair did we greet, and mickle did we say; weep; much
We took but ae kiss, and we tore ourselves
away:
I wish I were dead, but I'm no' like to dee:
O! why do I live to say, Wae's me!

I gang like a ghaist, and I carena to spin;
I darena think on Jamie, for that would be
a sin;
But I'll do my best a gude wife to be,
For auld Robin Gray he is kind unto me.

LADY ANNE BARNARD.

WILL YOU NO' COME BACK AGAIN?

ROYAL Charlie's now awa',
over — Safely owre the friendly main;
Mony a heart will break in twa,
Should he ne'er come back again.
not — Will you no' come back again?
Will you no' come back again?
loved — Better lo'ed you'll never be,
Will you no' come back again?

all; own — The hills he trod were a' his ain,
birch — And bed beneath the birken tree;
The bush that hid him on the plain,
There's none on earth could claim but he.
Will he no' come back again? &c.

Whene'er I hear the blackbird sing,
Unto the e'ening sinking down,
(here probably) thrush — Or merle that makes the woods to ring,
have no other sound — To me they hae nae ither soun',
Than, will he no' come back again? &c.

Mony a gallant sodger fought,
fall — Mony a gallant chief did fa';
Death itself was dearly bought,
A' for Scotland's king and law.
Will he no' come back again? &c.

lark's — Sweet the lav'rock's note and lang
Lilting wildly up the glen;
refrain — And aye the o'ercome o' the sang
Is, "Will he no' come back again?"
Will he no' come back again? &c.

LADY NAIRNE.